Wakefield Press

Yura and Udnyu

Peggy Brock is Emeritus Professor of History at Edith Cowan University, Visiting Research Fellow at the University of Adelaide and a Fellow of the Academy of Social Sciences in Australia. Since the 1980s, when the first edition of this book was published, she has written extensively on Indigenous responses to colonialism. Her most recent books are *Indigenous Evangelists and the Question of Authority in the British Empire* (co-author) and *Colonialism and It's Aftermath: A History of Aboriginal South Australia* (co-editor).

Yura and Udnyu

A history of the Adnyamathanha of the North Flinders Ranges

PEGGY BROCK

Wakefield
Press

Wakefield Press
16 Rose Street
Mile End
South Australia 5031
www.wakefieldpress.com.au

First published 1985
This revised edition copyright © Peggy Brock, 2019

Cover concept by Liz Nicholson, designBITE
Typeset by Michael Deves, Wakefield Press

ISBN 978 1 74305 673 8

NATIONAL
LIBRARY
OF AUSTRALIA

A catalogue record for this
book is available from the
National Library of Australia

This publication has been assisted by
the History Trust of South Australia –
Wakefield Press History Initiative.

HISTORY
TRUST
OF SOUTH
AUSTRALIA

Government
of South Australia

CORIOLE
McLAREN VALE

In the title of this history Yura means 'Aboriginal person' (or blackfellow, as the Adnyamathanha prefer) and Udnyu means 'white person'. Udnyu is also the word for 'dead': when the Adnyamathanha first saw white people they thought they were spirits of the dead.

Contents

Author's note 1985

Yura and Udnyu started life as a departmental report on the Adnyamathanha in the 1980s. Primarily, the history was recorded for the Adnyamathanha community and high school students, and was written with these readers in mind. Because of the interest in Aboriginal history amongst the general public, the book was adapted for a wider readership and published in 1985.

In the past there has been no standardised spelling of Adnyamathanha words. The word 'Adnyamathanha' has variously been spelt 'Anjamntina, Andyamatana, Unyamootha, Adnjamatana' (Norman B. Tindale, Aboriginal Tribes of Australia (Canberra, 1974), p. 219). I have adopted the orthography linguist Dorothy Tunbridge uses in *Artefacts of The Flinders Ranges; an illustrated dictionary of artefacts used by the Adnyamathanha.* Adelaide: Pipa Wangka, 1985.

Peggy Brock

Author's note 2019

When I was approached by Wakefield Press with the suggestion that *Yura and Udnyu* be republished I was faced with the dilemma: should it be republished as a facsimile in its original form or updated? This colonial history of the Adnyamathanha of the north Flinders Rangers was researched in the early 1980s and published 34 years ago. I decided it needed to be updated and the text revised so that it reflects changing knowledge and attitudes with a new chapter which would bring some of the major issues facing the Adnyamathanha in the twenty first century to the attention of readers. This is not a comprehensive survey of the Adnyamathanha today. I am sure there are many other issues and developments that could be raised, but to the historian the overwhelming change between 1985 and 2018 is the legal recognition of native title in Australia and the wide-ranging implications of that change in Australian law. The chapter '1973–2018 Self-determination and Native Title' considers how the Adnyamathanha have negotiated the changing administrative and political environment since the end of the mission days. The chapter is in two parts. The first outlines the major developments over the 40 years since the South Australian government took over the running of the United Aborigines Mission at Nepabunna; the second is Vince Coulthard's firsthand account of his life: growing up at Nepabunna, working in the pastoral industry as so many Adnyamathanha did before him and then gradually gaining knowledge and skills which have enabled him to become a key community leader helping to guide the Adnyamathanha through the complexities of the Native Title Act and the opportunities native title has presented in terms of control of traditional lands, cultural development, dispersement and investment of mining royalties and other funds, and negotiations with mining companies and government authorities. I would like to thank Vince and Gayle Mather from ATLA for making the time available for the extended interview with Vince and making available various publications from ATLA.

I would also like to thank Lea Gardam at the South Australian Museum and Suzy Russell at the State Library for their assistance in tracking down photos for this edition of the book.

Peggy Brock

List of illustrations

Foreword

The passing of the referendum of 1967, giving Aboriginal people full rights as Australian citizens, gave the Adnyamathanha people confidence to fight for their own rights to be equal in the Australian community. After a lot of agitation we won the right in 1973 to run our own community at Nepabunna in the Flinders Ranges. It had previously been a mission station controlled by the United Aborigines Mission. As a child growing up on the Nepabunna Mission in the 1950s and 1960s, I found that it was a very restrictive environment. The missionaries controlled our lives. For instance, they did not permit de facto relationships, we were limited in what we could say in our own language, parents did not have full control over their own children's upbringing and the missionaries interfered with our cultural life. The Adnyamathanha are now in full control of their own community and we are able to bring up our children the way we want.

A decision was made by the Adnyamathanha elders in the 1960s to share some of their knowledge of important Aboriginal sites with the general Australian community. The elders realised that this information might be lost as the last initiations were held in 1947–48 and the younger people were growing up without a knowledge of their heritage. At first the community worked with Bob Ellis, who at that time was Curator with Aboriginal and Historic Relics at the South Australian Museum. In the 1970s, four Adnyamathanha people, including myself, began working as rangers with Aboriginal and Historic Relics (which later became the Aboriginal Heritage Branch in the Department of Environment and Planning) recording our own people's oral history and important sites in the Flinders Ranges.

This recording program expanded to take on an educational role. The Adnyamathanha rangers began taking groups, mainly from schools, through the Ranges to show them non-sacred Aboriginal sites and explain why they are significant to Aboriginal people, and also to introduce these groups to the social and cultural life of the Adnyamathanha.

While the program of recording Aboriginal myths and sites continues, the Adnyamathanha wanted a record of our history since Europeans came onto our land and disrupted our traditional way of life. We wanted other Australians to know what happened to us and our land, and also so our children would have a written record of our history.

As I am now a cultural teacher seconded to Aboriginal Education in the South Australian Education Department, I am very aware of how little written material is available for teachers and students to learn about Aboriginal history and culture. I am pleased about this book being available for all Australians and particularly for school children and hope that there will be many more books written about other Aboriginal groups in the country.

I am very glad that a person like Peggy Brock was able to research this book, and the Department of Environment and Planning enabled her to do it. I know it was a lot of work going through the archives and finding information about the

Cliff Coulthard and Peggy Brock at the Nepabunna
80th anniversary celebration in 2011.

Adnyamathanha community, and it has also involved many
trips to the Flinders Ranges to talk to Adnyamathanha people
and record their memories of their history. Peggy has made
many good friends among the community and they respect the
work she has done and really enjoyed working with her. The
Adnyamathanha rangers in the Aboriginal Heritage Branch found
her easy to work with and a good friend.

I would like to thank the Adnyamathanha people for sticking
together to prepare a book like this, which is so important to our
culture and history, and I hope many people will take the time
to read it and look at the land through the eyes of Aboriginal
people and realise that as Peggy and I have worked together just
as people recording history, so all black and white Australians
should work together to record the history of Australia.

Cliff Coulthard, 1985

Introduction

Prior to the 1980s Australian history was primarily a history of colonial settlement in Australia, any references to Aboriginal people were incidental. More recently both Aboriginal and non-Aboriginal people have become aware of this imbalance and want it rectified. Many Aboriginal communities realise there is a gap in their knowledge of their own past. While knowledge of the myths and sacred life from the traditional, pre-European past is transmitted from generation to generation, less is known of the period of European settlement. This post-contact history is extremely important to Aboriginal people today because it both recounts and explains the significance of events in the living memory of the people. The researching and writing of Aboriginal history can result not only in the recording and interpretation of past events but also in relating them to the land on which they occurred. Historical research can therefore assist in the identification of areas of significance to Aboriginal people; such as campsites and religious sites, and since the 1990s it has been an important component of native title claims. Aboriginal people have always had close ties to the land and this should be recognised in the writing of their history. It is also important that non-Aboriginal people are aware of the colonial history that usurped the land and displaced the people who inhabited the continent, and that the repercussions of that process are still evident today.

While Aboriginal people share a history of dispossession, displacement, and disempowerment with high rates of disease and death, as well as economic, social and cultural disruption, these processes and lived experience vary from region to region. The first Europeans to visit the land and coastal waters of what is now South Australia were the sealers and whalers who arrived in the early nineteenth century before the colony of South Australia was established. They had settlements on Kangaroo Island and on the south-east coast of South Australia and made forays along the coast in search of Aboriginal women, whom they kidnapped and took back to their settlements. Some Aboriginal people in coastal regions, therefore, encountered the roughest elements of European society long before their land was formally colonised and taken from them.

Aboriginal people along the River Murray came in contact with exploring parties led by Charles Sturt in the 1830s. Sturt noted that diseases similar to smallpox and venereal syphilis were prevalent among the Aboriginal people he met.[1] These diseases were either communicated along the Murray from the eastern colonies or from the South Australian coast, where the sealers had made contact.[2]

When the colony of South Australia was established, Adelaide, the capital, expanded very rapidly and the fertile country around the city was quickly developed. Small towns grew up along the coast and in the hills behind Adelaide. The local Aboriginal people, the Kaurna, were displaced and dispossessed by this rapid influx of Europeans, and twenty years after settlement only a few members of this community survived.[3]

As South Australia developed, exploring parties moved out from Adelaide in search of agricultural and pastoral land. They were rapidly followed by settlers who took up the land, clearing it for agriculture and moving cattle and sheep on to land that looked suitable for grazing. Clearing land for agriculture had a more immediate impact on local Aboriginal people. It abruptly removed their traditional food supplies, both plant and animal, and the Aborigines' presence was considered incompatible with agriculture by the settlers. Many Aboriginal people who lived in these agricultural areas did not survive the intrusion of Europeans on to their lands. Those who did survive were herded together on to mission stations such as Point Pearce on Yorke Peninsula and Point McLeay on Lake Alexandrina. The government, through the Protector of Aborigines, established ration stations or depots to feed Aboriginal people whose traditional sources of food had been diminished. Distribution of rations through mission stations, Aboriginal schools, police stations and pastoralists was an effective way of controlling the movement of the Indigenous population. As rations were the only source of food and blankets for many of these people they tended to gather in the vicinity of these distribution points. As colonists discouraged Aboriginal people from congregating in towns, the ration depots were located outside townships. In the mid-nineteenth century when settlers complained Aboriginal people were attacking their stock, rations were distributed in pastoral areas prevent these attacks. Ration distribution in these regions had the added benefit of attracting a cheap labour force as recipients camped close to their source of food.[4]

The rations distributed by the Protector of Aborigines were basic, of poor quality, and not nutritious, unlike traditional food. They consisted of flour, tea and sugar, and sometimes tobacco and rice. No meat, vegetables or fruit were distributed. The rations were usually given to the old and sick, women and children and to those men who could not find work. Blankets were also distributed through ration depots, one blanket per person.

The impact of pastoralism on Aboriginal people was not as immediately devastating as urbanisation and agriculture. Pastoral leases allowed the free movement of Aboriginal people through the leasehold, and the impact on the natural environment was not as immediately destructive as other European activities. However, in the medium- to long-term the pastoral industry impacted on many aspects of traditional Aboriginal life. Pastoralists controlled the water sources, stock ate the grasses and plants which sustained local people and native game. In some regions the Aboriginal people adapted to their changed environment and survived as in the North Flinders Ranges; in a few regions, such as the northwest of South Australia, the people survived with minimal impact on their traditional life; but in other areas communities, such as the Dieri east of Lake Eyre, were virtually destroyed by the intrusion of outsiders.

The history of various Aboriginal communities in South Australia since European contact will, therefore, explain why different communities value different experiences in their past and why areas they have inhabited in historical times (the last 180 years) can be as important to them as campsites and religious sites of the distant past. This book recounts the history of the Adnyamathanha people of the North Flinders Ranges, whose response to the arrival of settlers on their lands has ensured the persistence of aspects of their pre-European culture and their survival as a coherent community.

1

The Adnyamathanha

Nepabunna settlement about seventy kilometres east of Leigh Creek is the home of the present day Adnyamathanha. It was established as a mission in the early 1930s by the United Aborigines Mission and in 1973 was taken over by the South Australian government for the Adnyamathanha who run the settlement through their own elected Council which is now part of the Local Government Association of South Australia. Nepabunna was not a traditional campsite; it is very rocky and the people in the past preferred camping on softer ground, so it was not their preferred location. But today it is very important to them, the place they consider home. It is central to their traditional lands and a place of refuge. The retention of a 'home' has enabled the Adnyamathanha to retain a cultural and linguistic identity which they might otherwise have lost.

The Adnyamathanha of today are descended from the Aboriginal peoples of the North Flinders Ranges. Adnyamathanha means 'hills or rock people'. The people who lived in the North Flinders Ranges at the time of colonial intrusion were the Wailpi, Kuyani, Yadliawarda and Pirlatpa (see maps on pages 6–7), and it is thought by some that a group called the Adnyamathanha

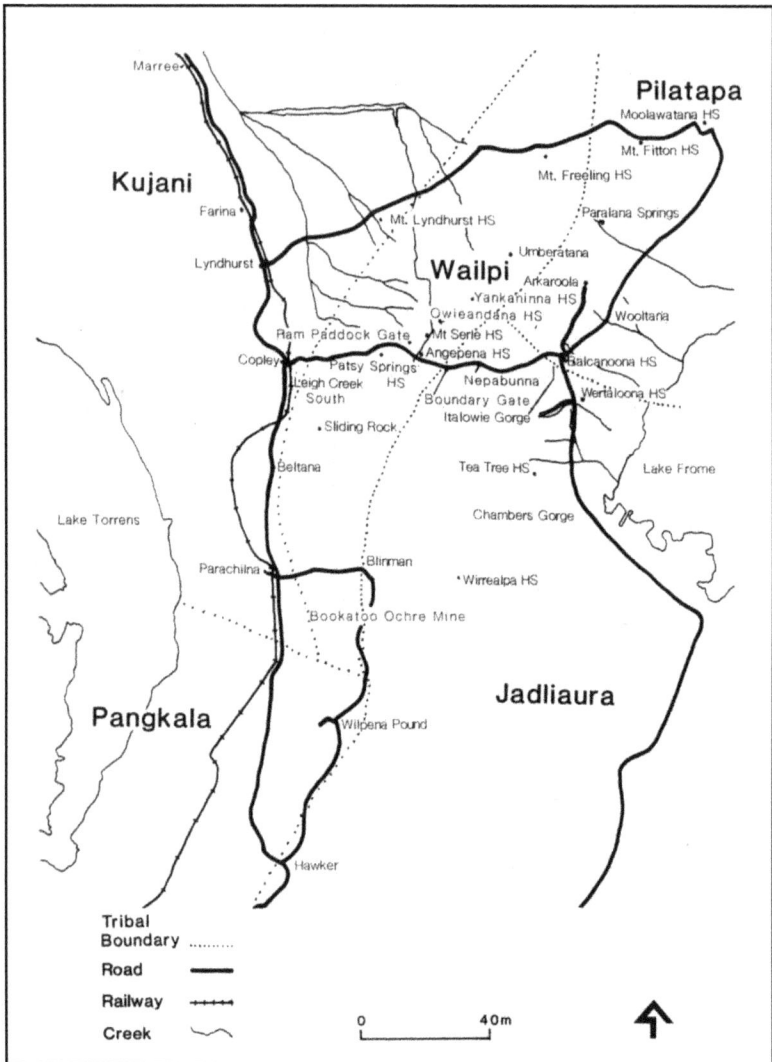

Pre-European tribal grouping based on Norman Tindale, *Aboriginal Tribes of Australia* (1974). Tindale says that the Adnyamathanha were not a separate tribal group, but the term merely referred to the people of the hills.

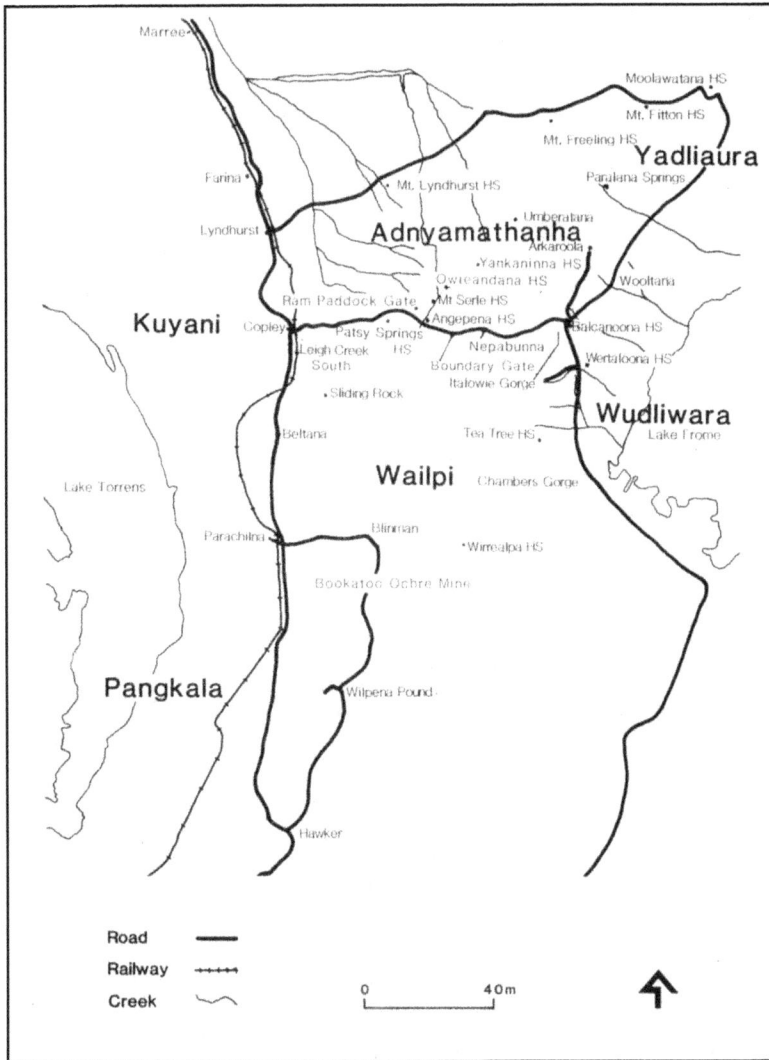

Pre-European tribal grouping based on the fieldnotes of C.P. Mountford (Mountford-Sheard Collection, State Library of South Australia), Mountford claimed that the Adnyamathanha were a separate tribal group from the Wailpi located to the north of them, and that Wailpi comes from the word for south, that is southern Adnyamathanha. Mountford also mentions a group between Lake Frome and the Flinders Ranges, the Wudliwara (*wudli* meaning 'other side', that is, the other side of the Range), not mentioned by other sources or informants.

7

existed on the western slopes of the Ranges.[2] The people of the North Flinders and the plains to the east and west spoke the same language (with differing dialects) and followed similar customs. It is thought by some that the different groups became subsumed under the one group name, Adnyamathanha, through intermarrying. Others claim that the groupings that existed prior to white invasion were so weakened by violent contact, disease and other destructive aspects of white contact that the remnants of these groups formed the larger Adnyamathanha group for survival. For example it is known that *wilyaru* initiation[3] was held at Mount Lyndhurst in the 1890s, at which Dieri, Arabana, Wailpi, Yadliawarda [Jadliaura] and even Wangkangurru [Wonguranda][4] (Oodnadatta region) were present. Rufus Wilton an Adnyamathanha elder born in the early twentieth century was told 300 to 400 people were at this large gathering, which was organised to enable an initiation to proceed despite the shortage of manpower in the various tribal groupings.[5]

Some of the Adnyamathanha know the earlier tribal associations of various families: the people from the Mount Serle area were Adnyamathanha; those from the Blinman area were Wailpi, people from Wooltana were Yadliawarda and those from Mount Lyndhurst were Kuyani (Guyani). These groups had their main campsites at different places, such as Wooltana, Mount Serle and Paralana.[6]

In pre-colonial times the Adnyamathanha were a mobile people, who moved from one camping place to another in the North Flinders Ranges in search of food and water, for ceremonial occasions, or because of a death in the camp. If a person died, people of the same moiety[7] as the dead person burnt the shelter and other things associated with the person, and moved to another campsite.[8] The Adnyamathanha also shared camping areas with other language groups.

Adnyamathanha had a complex and strict kinship system. It dictated how each member of the community could relate to every other member, for instance, it indicated to whom one could speak, with whom one had to avoid personal contact and who one could marry. The two basic groupings referred to as moieties, were Mathari and Ararru. A child belonged to the moiety of its mother. Anthropologists call this a matrilineal moiety system. A person had to marry someone of the opposite moiety, that is, a Mathari man could only marry an Ararru woman. Within each moiety there were totem groupings, which were generally associated with animals in different regions of the Adnyamathanha territory.

Mathari totem groups included: Yarlpumukunha from *yarlpu* (kangaroo rat) in the Mount Serle area; Warratyimukunha from *warratyi* (emu) in the Blinman area. Ararru totem groups included: Walhamukunha from *walha* (wild turkey) in the Mount Serle area; Mandyamukuhna from *mandya* (euro) in the Mount Serle area. Plants such as *minara* (bullock bush) and *urti* (wild peach tree) and the two winds *vadpa* (cold, south wind) and *vukarra* (hot, north wind) were also associated with totem groups.[9]

As with many other Aboriginal people throughout Australia, Adnyamathanha life and culture are closely associated with the natural environment. People knew where they, their parents and other relatives were born. They associated particular trees or camp areas with births or deaths in their community. Their mythology is also associated with land formations, plants and trees in their environment. Bob Ellis has given examples of how the destruction of the natural environment can also kill the mythology with which it is associated. The mythology gives meaning to cultural and social behaviour, the destruction of one element can lead to the destruction of other elements of Adnyamathanha life.

Ellis explains how the story of a large gum tree in Wilpena Creek provides a social justification for an unusual type of Aboriginal marriage. The destruction of the tree might result in the myth associated with it being forgotten:

> The story concerns old man Wirri who is the Moon. He was a greedy old man who used to take food from his nephews and who, furthermore, had two wives while his nephews had none. His nephews eventually decided to even with him and secreted witchetty grubs in a tall gum tree. They then went to see their uncle whom they called *namana* (mother's brother) – literally *nami-na* (male mother) – and told him they had discovered a tree rich with the grubs. Being a greedy man he decided to climb the tree and dig out the grubs which he threw down to his wives below the tree. However, while he was climbing the tree his nephews below were blowing on it and causing it to grow. He and his wives noticed this and his wives called for him to come down but he kept climbing and digging out more witchetty grubs. Eventually he was at the top of the tree and it touched the sky. His nephews called out to him to touch the sky but as soon as he did they pulled the tree down and left him in the sky. When he was thus imprisoned the two nephews stole his wives whom they called, according to kinship affiliation, *atapi* (father's sister) – literally *ata-vapi* (female father). This is why it is now possible in Adnyamathanha society to marry your *atapi* provided she is younger than you.[10]

Some traditional Adnyamathanha marriage rules are still followed, so although the Adnyamathanha now marry in the European style, the mythology can have a very direct impact on their lives.

2

1840–1870
The Establishment of
Colonial Settlement

The history of Aboriginal-European contact in the North Flinders began with bemusement on the part of the Adnyamathanha, followed by conflict (often violent) as the pastoralists moved in to claim land, and then a period of adaptation by the Adnyamathanha to the pastoral economy which dominated much of their lands.

Arrival of the Europeans in the North Flinders Ranges

E.J. Eyre was the first European explorer to travel through the North Flinders Ranges in 1840. He and his party were searching for land to pasture cattle and sheep. They were observed by local Aboriginal people, and stories of these first sightings of strangers have been handed down through the generations to the present. Adnyamathanha, who saw the first intruders in the Ranges, recounted these events to Angepena Billy and Mount Serle (King) Bob who died in 1919. They in turn passed these stories on to their children. One relates how an Adnyamathanha man hid when he saw the strange apparitions, only coming out to examine the strange horse tracks which he had never seen before. He continued to track the exploring party to their next camp site. A second story recounts that a group of Adnyamathanha had climbed a tree to collect witchetty grubs when they were assailed by an exploring party who showed them matches and tomahawks, but these strange goods created apprehension rather than curiosity. When the group came down from the tree they found the matches and tomahawk had been left for them, but they were too frightened to use the matches.[1]

Pastoralists moved into the North Flinders in the 1850s. J.F. Hayward stocked Aroona run in 1851, and by the mid-1850s pastoralists had moved to Angepena and beyond. As the settlers set up camps and ran their stock over Adnyamathanha lands, they destroyed much of the traditional Aboriginal food sources. The stock monopolised water supplies and grazing land, eating native plants which the Adnyamathanha had harvested for seeds and fruits, and competing with native fauna for food and water. In contrast with the increasing difficulties the Adnyamathanha had obtaining food from traditional sources, the pastoral camps appeared to have ready access to food, so the locals were inevitably attracted to these camps as they were set up often near traditional Aboriginal camping grounds close to precious water supplies. Owieandana was one of the main meeting points in the early days of European intrusion and it was there that the Adnyamathanha were first given rations and shown how to cook with flour.[2]

The main written sources of information about the earliest encounters between Adnyamathanha and colonists are reminiscences and diaries of early pastoralists in the Flinders Ranges. J.F. Hayward was overseer at Pekina station (east of Mount Remarkable) in 1847 and took up Aroona run in 1851. His diary is one of the few accounts of early settlement in the Flinders Ranges that has survived.[3] Life was rough and so were the interactions between the pastoralists and the Aboriginal people. Hayward and his neighbours considered the land was theirs and that the Adnyamathanha were the intruders with no rights. They considered the Aborigines used 'craft and cunning' to steal from and harass the pastoralists, and were outraged when on occasion, they even resorted to murder. Hayward did not consider that shooting and killing Adnyamathanha was murder.

In his diary Hayward recounts how he led a party of men in pursuit of a group of Aborigines, whom he believed had stolen some of his stock. He surprised them, but the men escaped each carrying a child. Hayward comments that the Aboriginal men knew the colonists never shot at women and children and so they used the children for cover. This, of course, implies that Hayward had no compunction about shooting Aboriginal men.[4] This impression, that many of the Aboriginal men in the Ranges were shot by pastoralists and their employees, is reinforced by John Bowyer Bull in his reminiscences.[5] Bull roamed over large areas of the colony of South Australia in the mid-nineteenth century in search of work and adventure. On one trip north delivering sheep to a station in the Flinders Ranges, he said he was surprised to see only black women. He asked the women where the men were and received the answer 'they said crackaback, dead ... all about white fellow shootam'.[6] Bull commented further that the Aborigines 'look upon the white man as their general enemy taking the water and hunting grounds from them and giving them no recompense for it, but shooting them down'.[7]

Despite this harassment and retaliation, Hayward and other pastoralists used Aboriginal labour to help them on their runs. Hayward points out that 'some of the black boys were quick to learn English and riding after stock and the men make capital trackers.'[8] Other pastoralists seem to have taken a more conciliatory approach with the local Aboriginal people and quickly became dependent on their labour. John McTaggart, who established Wooltana Run in 1856, employed Aboriginal labour and is said to have 'got on well with the natives ... he fought fair with the blacks with a waddy, not firearms'.[9] Nevertheless, this observation suggests violent interactions were accepted as normal only the level of violence varied.

By the mid-1850s ration stations were being established in the Flinders Ranges to feed the local people. As discussed earlier, when the Europeans moved in to an area and took over the land, they upset and sometimes wiped out traditional food and water supply. The local people then raided the introduced stock and colonists' huts for food. The government set up ration stations in an attempt to prevent these raids and as we have already noted used distribution of food as a means of controlling the movement of the Adnyamathanha, particularly in bad seasons.

The first police station and ration distribution point in the Flinders Ranges was at Mount Remarkable, now Melrose, followed by one on Angepena run. Where a hut keeper was killed near Mount Serle in 1856. J.B. Bull was working on an adjoining station and rode to Angepena to get a stockman, Stuart, to help him muster cattle. While at Angepena, Stuart took him down to the Aboriginal camp where they saw women and children who had been cut with stock whips. The women's breasts were cut open and little children of six to twelve months old were bleeding from whip cuts. Two stockmen on the Pernunna run had found the group at a spring and had attacked them while the men had taken another route hunting in the hills. When the men returned to their camp that night the stockmen believed they could hear them swearing and planning revenge. Despite this obviously explosive situation, Bull and Stuart set out next day to muster cattle leaving Mitchell, the hut-keeper, alone at Angepena. When they returned Mitchell was dead. Stockmen on neighbouring runs were outraged and frightened by this murder even though it was a provoked attack.[10] The circumstances of Mitchell's death were never transmitted south, only the fact of his murder and therefore the need for police protection from 'native outrages'.

The government's response to a call for a police presence in the North Flinders was immediate. A party of four police was despatched to catch the murderers and establish a police station near Mount Serle.[11] The police searched for the two main suspects in the murder of Mitchell, Puttapa Bob and Warranutta. Warranutta was captured, but escaped on the way down to Mount Remarkable, while Puttapa Bob was arrested. According to Bull, Puttapa Bob was surrounded by police and volunteers who fired on him for two hours. A trooper then knocked him down with a stone and he was found to have thirty shot wounds. He was then walked down to Mount Remarkable about 400 kilometres away. When Bull saw the prisoner at Mount Remarkable, the wounds crawling with maggots, he realised it was not Puttapa Bob, but an Aboriginal man named Peter, who died a few days later.[12]

Bull claims he never divulged this case of mistaken identity, his excuse being that the authorities were too inept to deal with it,

> I knew it was no use saying anything at that time to the inspectors or black protectors, as those men were always a lot of old women.[13]

However the authorities continued in the belief they had caught one of the murderers. On the second of March, 1857 a report from Mount Serle Police Station to Chief Inspector of Police, George Hamilton, warned there was a mob of twenty to thirty 'natives' who, having heard of 'Putaba' Bob's death, threatened to attack several stations including Angepena and stations to the north to drive all white men out of the North country.[14] This threatened attack never occurred because Mr Thomas, lessee of one of these stations, was said to have 'dispersed the natives' and they were not seen again.

The police made regular patrols around the Northern Flinders and on to the plains to the east and west. Their area of responsibility rapidly expanded over the ten years the police station operated. By the end of 1857 pastoralists Jacob, Randell, Gill and Swindon had moved to the eastern plain, north east of Mount McKinlay, to the western plain near Mount Deception and north beyond Mount Hopeless.[15] By March 1860 police patrols were going as far north as Blanchewater.

In the early years of the Mount Serle Police Station, the police were inundated with complaints about Aboriginal raids on sheep and cattle. The Adnyamathanha naturally hunted the stock which had replaced their traditional sources of meat such as euros, wallabies and possums. They did not understand nor acknowledge the European's concept of ownership. They only acknowledged their rights to the plants, animals, minerals and landforms which occur on their land. A specific area within the large group territory where an individual grew up, or where he or she had specific religious ties was regarded by that individual as his or her country because of the special intimacy that person had with the land and the responsibilities they had to nurture and look after the land and its resources. This relationship by individuals with specific areas of the Ranges is as true of Adnyamathanha people today as it was of their ancestors. The stock which replaced the native game on the pastoral land of the North Flinders Ranges and the plains to the east and west, was regarded by the Adnyamathanha as theirs in the sense that all animal life on their lands was regarded as theirs. The corporal in charge of the Mount Serle Police Station perhaps sensed this difference in attitude, but did not understand it. He commented that the blacks seemed to think they had as much right to the cattle as the pastoralists and that they often killed stock in the narrow gorges, but that they were unlikely to kill a hut-keeper or horseman unprovoked.[16]

Evidently, the Adnyamathanha had learnt very quickly to adapt their hunting techniques to new circumstances. They seem to have preferred catching sheep to cattle, as sheep were easier to catch. They could be disabled by breaking their legs and collected later. They also learnt to deal with cattle by herding them over cliffs or into narrow gorges, which had the added advantage of protection from the police and pastoralists. The colonists could not bring their horses up the narrow gorges and had to approach on foot. This made escape easier for the Adnyamathanha, who were much more adept at climbing the rough, rocky terrain and had the added advantage of being able to throw down rocks on their pursuers. The one or two-shot pistols, which the police carried, were relatively ineffective against Aboriginal people in this country. In October 1857, for instance, the police were called to Angepena station (owned by John Baker) after some cattle had been taken. Two police troopers accompanied by three other men tracked the Adnyamathanha and cattle to a gorge, tied up their horses and scrambled down the gorge three or four kilometres. They came upon twelve people with a large heap of meat. When the police party were twenty metres away, the Aborigines 'made up the rocks like wallabi'. After a police trooper fired at one of the men, he staggered, and the trooper tried to follow him. The injured man retaliated by throwing stones which almost killed the policeman. All escaped into the ranges. Subsequently it was discovered that only two head of cattle had been slaughtered.[17] The Aboriginal man who was shot may have been Wirrealpa Billy, an old man who died of his wounds.[18]

The authorities occasionally supported the Adnyamathanha in conflicts between pastoralists and their employees. When Mount Serle Police Station was first established the police found that on the plains where the Adnyamathanha had had longer contact with the settlers there was less conflict, except when they were 'annoyed' by hut-keepers and others 'by playing with and making much of them one minute and ordering them around the next'.[19] A report of trouble on McFarlane's run stated that McFarlane tried to force a man to do some work which he did not want to do. The black threw stones at McFarlane, and stones and waddies at his hut before going away.[20]

An incident which took place on John Jacob's property in 1858 is a good example of the confused attitudes many settlers had towards Aboriginal people during the period of conflict which arose as the pastoral industry expanded. Because food had been taken from a stockman's hut, the hut was never left unattended. Eventually the Adnyamathanha attacked the hut. One of the occupants escaped to get help while the other two were wounded and the hut was burnt. The police arrived and tracked the attackers with an Aboriginal 'tracker' and four volunteers to Arkaroola Creek. When the police caught up with them and asked them to stop, they threw stones at the police party. In retaliation the police fired and shot two of the Aboriginal men. The Mount Serle police were reprimanded by their superiors in Adelaide and told they were not justified by law in shooting Aborigines unless it was done in self-defence.[21] The police also arrested two men. One, Pompey, escaped, the other, Owieandana Billy was taken to Mount Remarkable. The Stipendiary Magistrate, Richard Minchin, refused to proceed with the case unless Jacob, or someone acting on his behalf, would come to Mount Remarkable to identify the prisoner and prosecute. After holding Owieandana Billy in custody for a month, while the police attempted unsuccessfully to collect witnesses, Minchin released the prisoner because no evidence was produced against him.[22]

Minchin defended himself against complaints made by police, producing a letter by Jacob explaining why he refused to prosecute.[23] Jacob argued that he would incur further losses by sending his men away to Mount Remarkable and leaving his property unprotected. His most experienced stockman was sure that the police had arrested the wrong person. He went on to say his overseer had no wish to shoot the Aborigines, which he might be forced to do if left to protect the station single-handed,

> The Natives have a great claim on our forbearance were it alone on the ground that we are as it were intruders on their country and the almost unavoidable consequences of the white man settling down there (to judge from previous experience) will be that in twenty years time, they will have become an almost extinct race, as where are now the fine tribes that were found in Adelaide as on the Murray in the early days.

Jacob recommended a less combative policy. On the suggestion of his overseer he had applied to the Commissioner of Crown Lands,

> to have some stores furnished by the Government to endeavour by a conciliatory system to obtain that influence over the Natives which, I hope, and trust will render unnecessary the being obliged to have recourse to measure which I should deeply regret and I would much rather submit to some losses than that

any lives should be sacrificed, and I am happy to say that the Commissioner had readily granted the request I made.[24]

However, Jacob's relatively enlightened attitude did not protect his cattle and sheep. In 1865 one of his shepherds was killed. His brother William Jacob then wrote to the Colonial Secretary asking that a 'protector of blacks' be placed in the north to reduce hostile feelings between the races,

> I pointed out to the Protector of Aborigines the boundary through which the more distant natives came into settled districts ... Over and over again have I urged that some steps should be taken, nay, even more, gone out of my way and suggested where the Government should long since have placed a Protector of blacks, if they really desired that any hostile feelings should be avoided between the races.[25]

The police could do little to intervene because the drought of the mid-1860s, which eventually drove both them and the Jacobs out of the area, was already well-established. The police had no horses suitable for riding because of lack of feed and water. The drought also explains the renewed attacks by Aboriginal people on stock, as food was as scarce for them as for police horses and policemen.

The drought must have had a devastating effect on the Adnyamathanha people, as the following extracts from a letter to the *South Australian Register* indicate.

> In ordinary years aboriginal natives have an ample supply of food in the numerous animals indigenous to this country. This year the terrible drought has been as fatal to those animals as it had been to the sheep and cattle of squatters,

The natural severity of the drought is greatly aggravated by the flocks and herds of the squatters which have utterly consumed or trodden out every vestige of grass or feed within miles of water. The aborigines have therefore but two resources – they are compelled to crowd around the dwellings of the squatters and beg for food or to follow the tactics of Rob Roy and prey upon their flocks and herds. If they adopt the first course the settlers cannot supply them ... if the natives adopt the alternative of helping themselves to food from flocks and herds of the settlers they are hunted by policemen, and if captured, are secured by a collar and chain rivetted around the neck and dragged away to stand trial under laws and customs they do not understand.[26]

The drought emphasised the disastrous effects the encroachment of the pastoralists on land in the North Flinders was having on Adnyamathanha society. Pastoralists and their employees regarded waterholes and springs as their property. On cattle runs they chased the Aborigines away from the waterholes because they claimed the Aborigines frightened off the cattle. The sheep trampled the ground around the waterholes preventing anything from growing there, and this affected the access native animals had to the water. Grazing also reduced the growth of the native plants on which the native animals and the Aborigines relied for food, leaving them dependent the sugar, flour and tea at ration stations. Poor diet and introduced diseases, to which the Aboriginal people had little resistance, killed many and maimed and crippled many more.[27] The Sub-Protector of Aborigines, J.P. Buttfield, who appears to have had no medical qualifications, treated many Adnyamathanha for what he called opthalmis, syphilis, rheumatism and chest and lung diseases.[28]

The introduction of the pastoral industry forced the Adnyamathanha to adjust their camping and movement patterns very rapidly to the changed circumstances. No land was specially set aside for them, although, in theory they were free to move over the pastoral leases, as Crown leases allowed free movement of Aboriginal people. In practice they were kept away from essential resources so established themselves in the vicinity of the homesteads where water, European food and work were available.

Despite the devastating attacks on their land and lifestyle the Adnyamathanha people survived the first years of contact, although many colonists were predicting that they must inevitably die out as so many Aboriginal people had before them.

The Ochre Trail

By the mid-1860s there were fewer reports of violent encounters between the Adnyamathanha and the settlers. Subsequent clashes were more likely to involve Aboriginal people from further north, often referred to as the Salt Water Blacks, from Lake Hope, Coopers Creek and around Lake Eyre. These people would make regular trips into the Flinders Ranges for ochre from the mines at Parachilna (Bookatoo mine) and the Aroona Hills. These mines produced high quality ochre which was used for body decoration and rock painting. It has a silvery sheen necessary in important ceremonies. Inferior quality ochre could be used on other occasions.[29] The ochre dust was collected, mixed with water and formed into large cakes (weighing around 30 kg) with an indentation to enable the miners to carry them on their heads over long distances. Aboriginal people came from as far away as southern Queensland and the Salt Lakes area of north-eastern South Australia. These people would gather in large groups as they went south for their ochre travelling in winter when water was more plentiful and they could travel longer distances without it. The expeditions were associated with initiation and other ceremonies. Permission was sought from the local Aboriginal people, the Wailpi, or possibly all the *wilyaru* (initiated) men of the North Flinders Ranges,[30] and trade in goods such as pituri (a plant which was chewed for its narcotic effect) from southern Queensland, green stone axes and flints was undertaken.[31] Women were on occasion also sent to the Adnyamathanha elders ahead of an ochre party. If outsiders came to the mines without permission they risked being attacked by the caretakers. Such an attack occurred in the mid to late-nineteenth century. The local Wailpi people, including Larrikin Tom, surrounded the mine and attacked the intruders as they came out.[32]

The establishment of the pastoral industry created new hazards and opportunities for people travelling to the ochre mines. Not only were the northerners moving through territory of other land-owning groups, but they now had to contend with the colonial presence of pastoralists. The travellers took advantage of the ready food supply on their trail south, killing cattle and sheep and raiding stockmen's and shepherds' huts. Settlers perceived them to be more aggressive and warlike than the local people. Their attempts to deal with this threat to their lives and property illustrates how little they understood Aboriginal culture and values.

The Chief Inspector of Police on a trip north in 1863, met a party of about 200 Aboriginal people on their way to Parachilna.[33] He first saw the party at Tooncatchin where they had stopped to perform an initiation ceremony. This group comprised people not only from the north-east but from the east and south as well. Later the police encountered about sixty of these people at Parachilna

Creek collecting red ochre. The Chief Inspector reported he heard few complaints of Aborigines robbing huts or molesting settler men and women, although there had been instances of cattle being slaughtered, and on one station a hut occupied by a woman and her two children and two unguarded camps had been robbed. These attacks were obviously unexpected as the proprietor of the station said he had sold all his arms to the Lake Hope pastoralists as he had no need of weapons.

The Chief Commissioner of Police decided to investigate the possibility of supplying the red ochre to the Lake Hope and Coopers Creek people nearer their home territories to stop them from travelling south and so protect the pastoral runs.[34] He obviously did not recognise the special qualities of the Parachilna ochre and the cultural meanings associated with the mining site and the ancient route to it.[35] Corporal Wauchop of Mount Serle Police Station pointed out that although the northern people had originally come down to procure red ochre, they now had an added incentive of plunder as well. He also pointed out that the Adnyamathanha living around Mount Serle went to Parachilna for their ochre and could not suggest deposits further north which might be suitable.[36]

Various sites where ochre was available were suggested to the Chief Commissioner. The Surveyor-General identified a deposit on Lake Eyre. Another suggestion was the Aroona Hills. Eventually tenders were called from persons willing to mine the ochre from Parachilna and cart it north. No one tendered, so ochre was mined in Adelaide and sent up to the Moravian Mission at Kopperamana.[37] The experiment was not a success for reasons already discussed: firstly, the Parachilna ochre was so prized for its high quality that people were prepared to travel long distances to procure it and were not interested in an inferior substitute;

secondly, the trip south to the ochre mines was not just to mine ochre but was associated with a range of ceremonies; and, thirdly, the ochre deposits themselves were sacred Aboriginal sites with important myths associated with them which would be desecrated by outside interference.

There are many accounts of confrontation between pastoralists and Aboriginal people on the ochre trail. An article in the *Port Augusta Dispatch* of 9 June 1882 recounts an incident sixteen or seventeen years previously in which eleven people were killed after pillaging a shepherd's hut on Beltana station and another forty to fifty were thought to have died of wounds on their trip back north to their own territory. An inquest was held and a verdict of justifiable homicide returned.

Another confrontation took place on the Stuckey and Elder property at Umberatana in 1864. The official report claims that a group of 'Salt Water Blacks', headed by Pompey were making their way south from Lake Hope, robbed several huts on Umberatana station and demanded provisions from a lone woman at the old station. They also killed an Adnyamathanha man named Bobby. Next morning the Adnyamathanha told Samuel Stuckey they feared the northerners were going to kill them all. Stuckey attempted to capture Pompey, but when Pompey tried to escape he was shot and killed.[38] The official report of Pompey's death did not contain all the details relating to the incident and may have got some of them confused. The Adnyamathanha version of the incident relates that Mount Serle (King) Bob and his brother had a fight in which Mount Serle Bob's brother was badly wounded. Pompey then moved in and killed Mount Serle Bob's brother. (Mount Serle Bob died in 1919.) The Adnyamathanha alerted the local pastoralist (thought to have been Noble,[39] not Stuckey) who shot Pompey.[40]

King Bob at Angorichina, 1907.
[AA338/1/35/88, SAM]

When Pompey escaped arrest after attacking a shepherd's hut on the Jacobs' property in 1858 he apparently moved north into Dieri country. It is not known for certain whether he was an Adnyamathanha man who was forced to move out of his own country.[41] Howitt, who spent time with the Dieri, knew of Pompey whose Aboriginal name was Inabuthina (Inabuthina could be either a Dieri or an Adnyamathanha word, although it is possible it is an attempt at the Adnyamathanha word *inamathanha*, meaning 'this mob of people'). Howitt described Inabuthina as a leading man in his tribe who had to escape the consequences of defending his country.[42] Inabuthina, or Pompey, is one of the few Aboriginal people in the North Flinders Ranges who is known to have put up a prolonged and concerted fight against the colonial intrusion on their lands in the mid-nineteenth century. For a period of at least six years from 1858 to 1864 Pompey harassed the pastoralists and their employees in the Ranges before he was shot. It is possible there were other such leaders, whose fight was not documented, and whose names have been forgotten.

In the same year Pompey was killed another incident illustrates how violence could be avoided. A large group of Aboriginal people were reported to be robbing huts on Leigh Creek and Mount Deception runs and had even raided a tent at Parachilna. Rather than confront the group, the pastoralists left freshly killed meat along their route and offered them flour if they kept away from their workers' huts.[43]

In 1869 J.P. Buttfield, the northern Sub-Protector of Aborigines, tried to prevent starving Dieri from attacking stock on the ochre trail by intercepting them with a wagonload of provisions, however, he missed them.[44] The following year he was more successful. After reports of huts being robbed and sheep killed on the route through Beltana, Nilpena, Ercowie and Aroona runs, Buttfield took rations to Beltana where 150 people were camped. With the assistance of a local policeman he distributed rations and promised to issue more for their return journey.[45]

While the Chief Commissioner and authorities could attempt to alter the route or behaviour of the travelling ochre parties, they could not persuade pastoralists to modify their behaviour by moving their stock away from the known routes or putting them under heavier surveillance when an ochre party was expected. A common colonial story where the Indigenous population must accommodate the intruders on their land, rather than the colonists making compromises.

Parties from the north continued to collect ochre from the Parachilna mines well into the twentieth century. They even made use of the railway which extended to Marree by 1884 to facilitate their journey to the Ranges.[46] By the early twentieth century the ochre mine was under threat from colonial mining interests which created consternation among both the local Adnyamathanha and those further afield who collected ochre from Parachilna. They approached Dr P.F. Shanahan in Hawker in 1904 who wrote on their behalf to the Protector of Aborigines, Hamilton, and to Dr E.C. Stirling, the Director of the Museum, warning that the local Aborigines were concerned that the mines were to be taken over by whites and that this would result in reprisals both among Aboriginal people and against settlers in the outback. He suggested an area of only eight hectares would need to be reserved for the Aborigines to keep the precious mines in Aboriginal hands.[47]

This was followed by another submission emphasising the importance of establishing a reserve at the ochre mines. The Adnyamathanha were concerned that settlers were going to work claims there. A great gathering of Aborigines was planned in Brachina Gorge near the mines where the issue was to be discussed and it was suggested the Protector of Aborigines should go up and meet the 'King' of the tribe. The 'King' had warned that if the area was not reserved there were likely to be reprisals against whites in the far north.[48] In 1905 the government did reserve an area in Parachilna from the operation of the Mining Act 1893.[49]

By the 1880s confrontation between Aboriginal people in the Flinders Ranges and settlers seems to have dissipated. Those

Aboriginal people who survived the early years of violence, disease and the upheaval of their traditional life adapted to the pastoral economy, which now dominated the Flinders Ranges, and the sporadic mining activity, which did not become firmly established in the Ranges until the Leigh Creek coalfields were mined by the Electricity Trust of South Australia in the 1940s.

3

1870–1920s
The Adnyamathanha and the
Pastoral Economy

The physical environment of the Flinders Ranges in the late nineteenth century and early twentieth century had changed dramatically from the time when it had been inhabited solely by the Adnyamathanha. The pastoral industry was now well established. Native animals had to compete with the introduced cattle, sheep and rabbits. The countryside was dotted with small mines, which, although they only affected limited areas, often intruded on sites of special significance to the Adnyamathanha. Many of these European mining sites are important in Adnyamathanha mythology. Minerals are often associated with unusual geological formations and coloured rocks and earth whose existence is explained by the wanderings of mythological ancestors. For instance, the copper mines at Yudnamatana are associated with the story of Yadnamathanha, the witchdoctor, who hunted carpet snakes instead of wallabies. The rocks along which the witchdoctor dragged the carpet snakes have traces of green, the colour of copper.[1] The coal deposits at Leigh Creek are explained in the myth of Yurlu Yurlura, the kingfisher man, who came from the west in Guyani country and moved through the Flinders Ranges to Wilpena Pound. On his travels he lit a signal fire at Leigh Creek to let people know he was coming. The charcoal remaining from his fire formed the coal deposits at Leigh Creek.[2]

The Adnyamathanha now co-existed with the intruders, their values and their economy. This they succeeded in doing, although at great loss to their health, and the survival of individual members of their community. The survival of the Adnyamathanha community may be partly due to their incorporation of children of mixed unions as full members of their own society. The Adnyamathanha, as with other Aboriginal communities, had complex and very strict kinship rules. Contravention of these rules could result in the death of the wrongdoer.

These rules did not apply to sexual relationships with Europeans. Children born from sexual encounters between Adnyamathanha women and European men were accepted and brought up by the Adnyamathanha community. When the mother subsequently married an Adnyamathanha man he accepted the children as his own. There is no early record of children of a white mother and Adnyamathanha father. The first recorded marriage was between an English woman Rebecca Castledine and Jack Forbes in the 1920s. Such marriages are quite common today and the children are considered part of the community.

Occasionally the non-Adnyamathanha fathers tried to gain control of their children through police action, for instance the Beltana police attempted to 'arrest' children as neglected and bring them under State control. However, in two documented cases the mother and stepfather refused to give up their children and it was subsequently found they were not neglected as their stepfathers had employment.[3]

From the 1890s there were attempts by the colonial authorities to remove children of mixed descent from their families and send

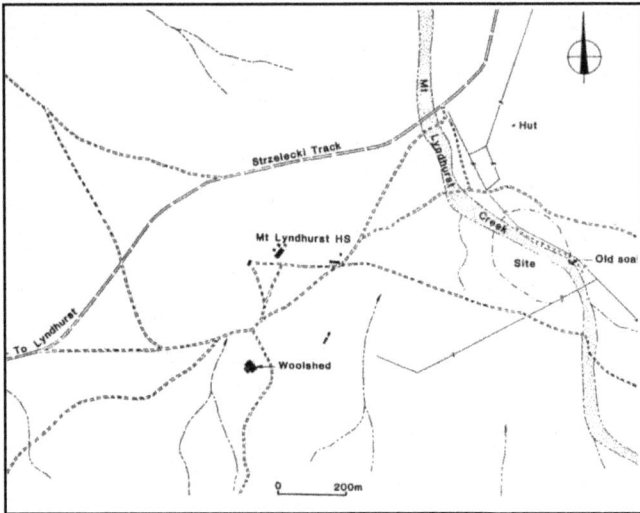

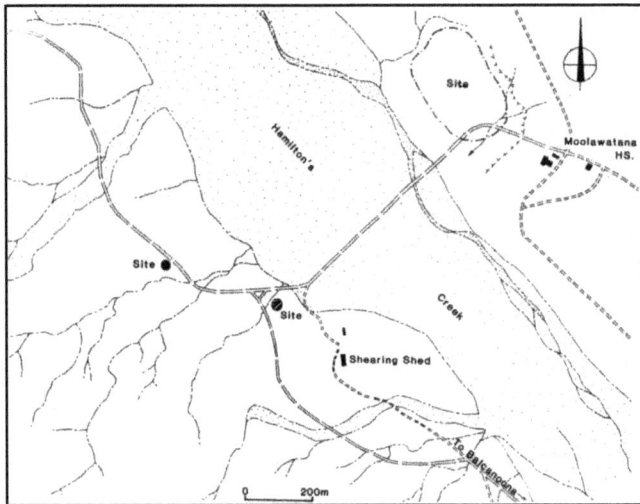

Aboriginal campsites in the North Flinders Ranges in the late nineteenth and early twentieth century. The establishment of the pastoral industry influenced the location of Aboriginal campsites. Homesteads had dependable water supplies and were a source of work and food, so most Aboriginal camps tended to be within a few hundred metres of a homestead.
Top: The campsite near the Mount Lyndhurst homestead. The people camped by a soak in the creek bed. *Bottom:* The campsite near Moolawatana homestead.

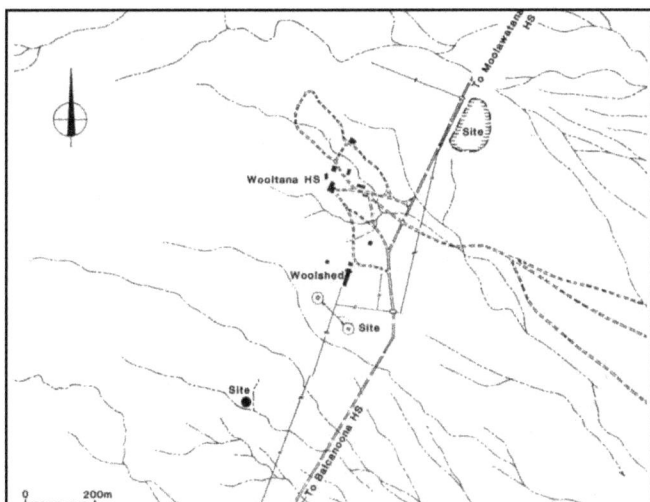

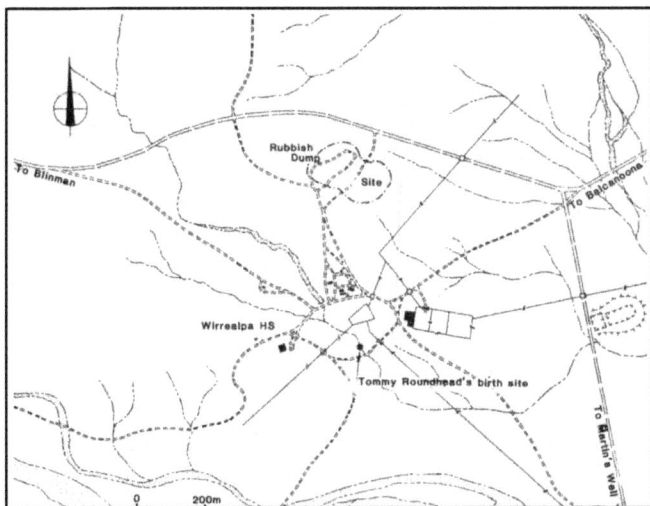

Top: The campsites near Wooltana homestead. The sites to the south of the homestead were occupied as recently as the 1960s.
Bottom: The campsites near Wirrealpa homestead.

Jack and Rebecca Forbes and children in front of a shelter
at Wooltana station.

[SAMA1083/39/7558, SAM]

them to mission stations. The Adnyamathanha managed to resist
these interventions by the Protector of Aborigines and police to
disperse their people. In 1893 the Sub-Protector of Aborigines
tried to take young children away to mission stations, but the
community would not allow them to be removed to regions with
different customs and languages.[4] In 1902 there was another
concerted effort by colonial authorities to send children to Point
McLeay near Lake Alexandrina. Families where one parent was
widowed were approached and encouraged to let their children
go. Henry McConville, a pastoralist in the Mount Serle area, who
seems to have been more attuned to Adnyamathanha sensitivities
than most colonists, pointed out that tribal laws prevented
parents from giving consent to the removal of their children.[5]
However, it was a measles epidemic that year which killed at least
eight adults that finally ended efforts to remove Adnyamathanha
children from their devastated community.[6]

Sydney Ryan, his wife and sister-in-law in front of their shelter.
[SAMA1083/31/5764, SAM]

Most of the camps of the Adnyamathanha were near colonial settlements. These settlements included homesteads on pastoral runs: Moolawatana, Paralana, Mount Serle, Frome Well (Angepena), Mount Lyndhurst, Owieandana, Mount Freeling, Burr Well (Depot Springs), Wooltana, Balcanoona, Umberatana, Wirrealpa, Mount Fitton, Beltana and Wertaloona; or near mines, such as Yudnamatana; or in the vicinity of townships, such as Blinman. Some of these sites coincided with traditional campsites, others did not. They were chosen primarily because they were near sources of employment, water and food. Mount Serle was the main gathering place for the Adnyamathanha at this time. When the police from Beltana took periodic censuses of the Aboriginal population, they visited Mount Serle and Frome Well. This gave them an indication of how many people were in camp at the time, but gave them little indication of the total Adnyamathanha population. Below are extracts from some of the censuses taken in the 1890s.[7]

1894–26 Aborigines at Mount Serle, 9 at Frome Well (some of the people were away shearing)

> 18 able-bodied men and women
> 10 old and infirm men and women
> 11 children

1896–67 Aborigines at Mount Serle

> 19 men
> 24 women
> 24 children

1897–11 Aborigines at Mount Serle

> 2 men
> 3 women
> 6 children

1898–38 Aborigines at Mount Serle, Frome Well and Angepena

> 18 able-bodied men and women
> 3 old and infirm men and women
> 17 children

The locations of ration depots changed from time to time depending on where the Adnyamathanha people were camping most frequently, and whether the local pastoralist was prepared to distribute rations. In 1894 the official ration depots were at Blinman, where the police distributed the rations, and on the pastoral runs at Beltana, Mount Lyndhurst, Mount Serle and Paralana.[8] Dependence on rations was governed by the seasons. In a good season only the old and infirm were reliant on rations, while the able-bodied were able to hunt game and collect fruits and seeds. There was also plenty of employment enabling them to buy the European food to which they had become accustomed.

Station work was a major source of employment, but for many of the Aboriginal stockmen it was seasonal work and in dry seasons there might be no work at all. Other work available in the Ranges was hunting dingoes and rabbits for which they were paid per scalp by the pastoralists, hunting kangaroos and euros for their skins, mining, working at the Mount Serle Camel Depot when it was established in the late 1890s, and collecting acacia gum which was used for making glue.

In dry seasons the Adnyamathanha were now very vulnerable, as they no longer had access to the water holes and springs they depended on in pre-European times. Native game had to compete with stock for food and water and became very scarce in bad seasons. There are reports of Aborigines starving in dry seasons. These people were classified as able-bodied and, therefore, not eligible for rations despite the scarcity of food.[9] In times of drought their situation was desperate.

During a prolonged drought in the 1890s, many runs were forced to close down. It was almost impossible for Adnyamathanha men to obtain employment during the drought. Everyone was also looking for alternative employment as station work became scarce. White station employees were shooting the wild dogs and poisoning the rabbits, work Adnyamathanha had previously undertaken, but they could not compete with settlers who had rifles for hunting game, while the Aboriginal people relied on waddies and their dogs. The only source of work left for them was catching dingo pups for which they received rations, not cash, a form of payment they resented.[10] They also collected gum for which they earned one penny per pound which was hardly enough money to sustain them.[11]

The condition of the Adnyamathanha during this drought in the North Flinders horrified many who saw them. It even prompted someone who basically lacked sympathy for Aboriginal people ('I do not hold the blacks up as being anything more than lazy, useless beings') to write to the *South Australian Register* in their support. This correspondent pointed out that the issuer of rations at Blinman, the local police trooper, was instructed not to issue rations to able-bodied men and he went on to say:

> Any person seeing the condition of so-called 'able-bodied' men would have been filled with disgust for the powers that be ... who are living upon the products of the soil taken from these unfortunates.[12]

The policeman from Beltana went to investigate conditions at Mount Serle reporting that while they had not received rations for several days, the people were not starving. He described them as too lazy to catch wallaby despite their explanations that they had no shot or nets to catch game and their dogs were too weak to run. He assessed their condition as good, notwithstanding the death of three women and a youth in the previous months.[13]

McConville on Angepena run was much more empathetic towards the dire conditions facing the Adnyamathanha. He said the drought was so severe there was no game in the Angepena hills. The people were close to starvation and had been forced to move camp because there were no rations, leaving two old women and two children behind. He pointed out that two years previously when Angepena, Artimore and Mount Serle runs were stocked, the young men had employment and supported the old ones, but the runs were now abandoned because of the drought.[14]

When Mount Serle run was abandoned the Government set up a Camel Depot on part of the run and put a caretaker, A.J. Strother, in charge who also became the issuer of rations. Strother was soon complaining about his job, calling the people 'bold and threatening', 'lazy and independent'. He said they refused to work for rations and demanded outrageous rates of

Women and children at Mount Serle ration depot, 1910.

[GN1315 South Australian Government Photographic Collection,
History Trust of South Australia]

Women queuing for rations at Mt Serle ration depot in 1910.

[GN13717 South Australian Government Photographic Collection,
History Trust of South Australia]

Women and children at Mt Serle ration depot in 1910 wearing ration blankets which are also used for carrying young children.

[GN13716 South Australian Government Photographic Collection, History Trust of South Australia]

Women and children at Mt Serle ration depot in 1910 by a bough shelter.

[GN13716 South Australian Government Photographic Collection, History Trust of South Australia]

pay. He was offering them 10 shillings per week and they were asking for £1 per week and double rations. When the policeman from Blinman went to investigate the complaints he found the people at Mount Serle of 'the same type and standard' as those of Blinman, Beltana, Wooltana and Port Augusta. He suggested Strother was lacking in sympathy and did not understand that he was living among Aborigines who had worked and lived amongst whites all their lives and that they were 'dependent on whiteman's tucker'. He also pointed out that there was no work available at any wage and that the people preferred buying rations when work was available to accepting Government rations.[15] Strother like his predecessor at Mount Serle wanted to close the ration depot, but, the Protector of Aborigines pointed out that the Adnyamathanha would not move away from their own country to be closer to other ration stations: firstly because Aboriginal people were very attached to their land; and secondly they would not be accepted by neighbouring people at Beltana or further afield.

Strother's complaints of Adnyamathanha attitudes and behaviour highlight the Adnyamathanhas' familiarity with the colonial world. They understood that settlers were paid higher wages than Aboriginal people and they wanted equal wages.[16] They knew government rations were issued free and resented it when the issuer demanded they work for them, yet by the 1890s they had become at least partly dependent on European food.

The following brief biographical sketches based on interviews with Adnyamathanha elders give an indication of the lives of the Adnyamathanha in the early and mid-twentieth century.

Cecil Stubbs known as Bill, was the son of an Adnyamathanha mother, Emily, who was born at Mount Rose and a white man, Benjamin Stubbs, who had come to the North Flinders in search of gold. Benjamin later returned to the south and ran a tree nursery in the Adelaide Hills. Bill was born about 1890 at the Ring Neck Tree on Mount Lyndhurst station near the windmill and tank. His sister was born at Yankaninna. When the children were very young, Emily worked as a cook on Mount Lyndhurst station and brought food home for the two children. The station was a ration depot at the time. When the family were on the move Bill carried the swag. Later Emily married Nicholas Demell at the gum tree on the creek on the road between Angepena and Mount Serle. Emily and Nicholas had four children. The family moved around the Ranges living at Mount Serle, Angepena, Depot Springs and Yudnamatana Mines. When Bill was old enough he worked on the stations. He camped out when doing station work moving where the work took him.

In 1928 Bill married Mabel Johnson at Ram Paddock Gate. After his marriage, Bill worked at Wooltana, Balcanoona, Wertaloona, Angepena and at Mount Serle, where he was breaking in camels. Bill and Mabel had two daughters. When the girls were old enough to go to school the family moved to Blinman where Mabel had a job at the pub and they rented a house from her boss. Bill worked on the roads. Later they moved to Nepabunna.

Rufus Wilton was born about 1910 at the Mount Serle Camel Depot. His father, George Edington, was the manager of the Depot. His mother Susan later married Albert Wilton. The police attempted to take Rufus away from his mother at his father's direction but his mother used to paint him with black ochre so he would look as dark as the other children. When the family was at Mount Serle they camped at the Bullock Bush near the homestead.

Rufus taught himself to read and write with some help from a pastoralist, Alf William, at Depot Springs. Rufus remembers in his youth that when the people moved camp they always cleaned

Rufus and Ethel Wilton, late 1930s.
[PRG1218/34/822, Mountford Sheard Collection, SLSA]

up the site so they could move back later. They burnt the wurlies and took everything else with them. They moved in circles because they had to keep close to the wells. Their diet consisted of government rations, damper, and game which they hunted, including euros, rabbits, wallabies and, at Angepena, possums. The old women would collect seeds when they were on the plains, for instance at Wooltana, and grind them on a large rock.

Rufus married Ethel Demell at Copley and they had eight children. Rufus worked on pastoral stations, including Mount Serle, Umberatana, Wirrealpa, Wooltana, Balcanoona and Mount Fitton. During this time his family lived at Ram Paddock Gate and later Nepabunna. He then worked at Leigh Creek for thirty years from the 1940s while the family rented a house from an Afghan at Beltana (as they could not get accommodation in Leigh Creek township).

Claude Demell was born in 1908 at Angepena. His parents were Emily and Nicholas Demell; Bill Stubbs was his stepbrother. Claude began station work in 1920. He worked at Depot Springs, Wertaloona, Mount Serle, Balcanoona and for the Beltana Pastoral Company.

Claude married Ethel Ryan in 1937. The family lived at Nepabunna and Beltana while Claude worked on the stations. He had no permanent dwelling when out working and received cooked meals from the homesteads. In 1958 the family moved to Blinman, while Claude continued to work on stations, and in 1962 they moved to Quorn so that the children could go to high school.

Pearl McKenzie was born in 1922 at Burr Well station. Her father Henry Wilton was born at Mount Serle, her mother, May, at Burr Well station. Both May and Henry grew up at Mount Serle station. Henry worked as a station hand at Burr Well and Wertaloona stations, returning to Mount Serle between jobs. They moved to the Adnyamathanha camp at Ram Paddock Gate for a few months and later to Nepbunna. During the Depression, Henry got occasional work at Balcanoona fencing and crutching sheep and later returned to work at Burr Well station. Henry and May Wilton had few possessions, a few cooking utensils and a swag, and were therefore very mobile. They would set up camp in traditional camping areas as they moved from station to station in a landscape which had personal meaning to them marked by their birth trees, marriage tree and graves of members of the family.

Pearl married John McKenzie in 1941 at Nepabunna and they went to Wirrealpa station where John worked as a station hand

Pearl Wilton, late 1930s.
[PRG1218/34/757B, Mountford Sheard Collection, SLSA]

and boundary rider and did some fencing. John also worked at Wertaloona station, and Martins Well. While John worked on the stations, and Pearl was at home alone, they were always given a house to live in on the stations, except for Wertaloona where they lived in the shearers' quarters. They had five children. In 1964 the McKenzies moved to Hawker. John worked as a professional kangaroo shooter for Jesser Chiller, and from 1970 he worked on the roads.

John and Pearl McKenzie, Claude Demell, Rufus Wilton and Bill Stubbs lived through the period that spanned the establishment of Nepabunna Mission. Their childhoods were similar to their parents', but during their adult lives they had more ready access

John McKenzie late 1930s.
[PRG1218/34/800B, Mountford Sheard Collection, SLSA]

to European housing, education for their children and regular wage labour. They moved around less frequently and were able to accumulate possessions.

The economic base of the Adnyamathanha of the late nineteenth and early twentieth centuries changed from one which was totally self-sufficient and reliant on the natural environment, and trade with other Aboriginal groups, to one which was dependent on colonists for paid work and rations. They generally dressed in European clothes, except when attending ceremonies. Housing resembled traditional living conditions, although the wurlies were not made of traditional materials, but a mixture of traditional and European products, including iron, kerosene tins and various types of cloth. Their diet was also a mixture of old and new: government rations, native seeds and fruits, native animals and introduced animals. They learnt new skills such as the handling of horses, camels, donkeys, cattle and sheep, and gradually lost some of their traditional skills such as hunting with spears and waddies. They learnt to speak English but retained Adnyamathanha as their first language. They were given no formal European education – Rufus Wilton was one of the few Adnyamathanha of his generation who learnt to read and write. On the other hand they retained their own pattern of social relations with regard to kinship, marriage, birth, death and the mythology and ceremony which accompanied it. They all had Aboriginal names, although they were known to settlers and even among themselves by European names. At first they were given first names by the pastoralists, generally in the diminutive such as Billy, Jimmy, Bobby. To distinguish them from others of the same name, they were given place names as well: Owieandana Billy, Frome Charlie, Beltana Bobby. By the late nineteenth century they were adopting European surnames, although how they came by their names is often not known. The Demells took their name from an Indian hawker, Peter Demell, who was killed by an Adnyamathanha man, although there seems to have been no blood connection with him. The McKenzies took their name from a Scotsman who had a relationship with an Adnyamathanha woman. The Wiltons and Coulthards seem to have been given their names by pastoralists and no doubt this is true of most of the surnames of present day Adnyamathanha people.

Ted Coulthard, late 1930s.
[PRG1218/34/760B, Mountford Sheard Collection, SLSA]

Some of the Adnyamathanha men were not only employed by whites but ran their own businesses. Ted Coulthard is probably the best known of these. He owned a team of donkeys at Mount Serle station which he later took to Ram Paddock Gate and Nepabunna. He used the team to bring in stores from Copley and cart fencing materials and other supplies. In 1924–25 he won a contract from the Vermin Board to build the netting fence (dog fence) in the Mount Serle area. This provided employment for many of the Mount Serle people including the Wiltons, Coulthards and the Ryans.

In 1923 the Camel depot was closed at Mount Serle and moved further south and 'Smiler' Greenwood took up the lease of the station and stocked it with sheep. The Greenwoods continued to issue rations until they had an argument with the Aborigines Department and refused to continue the service. The Adnyamathanha also realised that their stock and dogs were incompatible with the Greenwoods' sheep and so they moved off the property to Minara Vutu, also known as Ram Paddock Gate.

4

1931–1973
Nepabunna Mission

The move from Mount Serle to Minara Vutu (Ram Paddock Gate) in the mid 1920s was the beginning of another period of uncertainty and insecurity for the Adnyamathanha. The settlement which evolved at Ram Paddock Gate was near the boundaries of several stations including Burr Well, Mount Serle, Manners Well and Angepena, but was on Coles' and Whyte's property of Burr Well. The pastoralists did not welcome the Aboriginal community camped on their land fearing their stock and dogs would interfere with their own stock.

Nevertheless, the Adnyamathanha remained at Ram Paddock for several years. They built themselves houses of wood and stone with chimneys and roofs of flattened kerosene tins.[1] There was a burial site for each moiety, Ararru and Mathari, a well built on a traditional soak, and ceremonial sites where initiations and other ceremonies were performed. The Adnyamathanha were able to maintain a lifestyle here which incorporated traditional activities while participating in the colonial economy. It is estimated that over a decade at least 100 Adnyamathanha lived in the settlement, many people were buried there and up to six initiation ceremonies were held during that period.[2]

In 1929 Jim Page a United Aborigines Mission missionary joined the settlement and built a house for himself and a church. He issued rations to the people who had had to fend for themselves since the Greenwoods stopped issuing them at Mt Serle. Coles and Whyte became more determined to move the people off their land and sent angry letters to the Protector of Aborigines' office and Jim Page. The appearance of a second missionary, Fred Eaton probably further exacerbated the conflict with the pastoral lessees. Eaton was a carpenter by trade and had worked on stations in the North Flinders. He had previously had a disagreement with Whyte who employed him at Frome Station and called in the Australian Workers Union over a wages dispute.[3] The Adnyamathanha were willing to move, but they had nowhere to go. Pastoralists Waterhouse and Martin did not want them on their property at Manners Well. The government dragged its feet in trying to negotiate a reserve for the community. Finally the missionaries negotiated with Roy Thomas of Balcanoona station for some land near the Nepabunna Rockhole. By this time Whyte and Coles had threatened that they would visit the camp with the police and shoot all the stock de-pastured on their land. Ted Coulthard wrote two letters to the Protector of Aborigines in December 1930 and January 1931 asking for assistance in establishing themselves at Ram Paddock Gate, or some other site after Whyte and Coles threatened their stock. The community moved from Ram Paddock Gate to Boundary Gate (see map on p. 7) while negotiations were being concluded with Thomas. Ted Coulthard who was working on the Telegraph line from Beltana to Balcanoona resolved the impasse by asking for land in lieu of payment from Thomas. He received the land which is now the location of Iga Warta, which was later extended.[4] Finally, the Adnyamathanha had access to land on condition that:

- The land be fenced with a six-wire sheep and donkey proof fence.
- The main camp and Mission station not be situated near the Angepena boundary.
- The 'Native camp' be administered so as not to inconvenience the donor.
- Dogs be kept in check and that Thomas have the right to shoot any dogs or stock which stray on his property.
- A well be sunk by the Natives on MacKinlay Pound (part of the land donated).
- The land revert to the lessee should the United Aborigines Mission abandon the Mission.[5]

In 1931 the Adnyamathanha moved to Nepabunna which has since remained the central focus of their community.

The UAM missionaries ran the community from 1931 to 1973 when the government took control of Nepabunna. Jim Page and

Leather items made at Nepabunna, late 1930s.

[SAMA1083/9/1780, SAM]

Rufus Wilton sewing boots, late 1930s.
[SAMA1083/9/1780, SAM]

Fred Eaton established the Mission and, after Page's death in 1935, Mr and Mrs Eaton ran the Mission with assistance from others including Mr and Mrs Reisenbach, Miss Frazer (a trained nurse who taught the children for a few years) and Mr and Mrs R.M. Williams. Williams set up a leather workshop in a brushwood hut and claimed the industry was supporting eleven people in 1933.[6] But the UAM would not allow him to continue his workshop unless the money went back to the UAM.[7] In 1934 Williams left the Mission, having started an industry which was to become the multimillion dollar business of R.M. Williams Bushman's Outfitters.

The Eatons ran Nepabunna Mission until the early 1950s when Mr and Mrs Hathaway took over. Eaton is remembered by the people as a humane man who fought for their rights, although in a paternalistic way. He worked tirelessly to establish the Mission, sinking wells and building houses and fences. He also tried hard to establish some independent economic base for the community by establishing mining ventures and trying to obtain more land on which to run stock. He also strongly supported Ted Coulthard in his mining ventures. However, Eaton did not approve of the Adnyamathanha performing the second part of the initiation ceremony and, according to the anthropologist, Charles Mountford, Eaton used the threat of the UAM withdrawing and the Adnyamathanha losing their home, Nepabunna, if they did not conform to his wishes.[8] The Hathaways seem to have been less easy-going; they were more distant in their relationship with the Adnyamathanha people and appeared less tolerant of some other aspects of the people's traditional culture. For example they forbade the people to speak the Adnyamathanha language in front of them and penalised them if they did. They have also been blamed by some for ending the initiation ceremonies, although these in fact had stopped before the Hathaways came to Nepabunna. The Hathaways were not able to deal with the practical day-to-day running of the Mission as competently as Eaton, so that under their control the Mission became increasingly run down.

In 1966 people from the Nepabunna community wrote to the Aborigines Department asking the government to take over the Mission.[9] They complained of the continuing shortage of water and of inadequate and rundown housing, and demanded the freedom to run their own community free from any petty tyranny of the missionaries. In 1973 the government finally took control of the Mission and today the Adnyamathanha have freehold title of the Nepabunna land still mediated through the Aboriginal Lands Trust.

Life at Nepabunna in the missionary period 1931–73 developed a distinctive character and the settlement became the hub of Adnyamathanha life.

Housing

The establishment of Nepabunna Mission meant relative security after many years of uncertainty for the Adnyamathanha community. They worked with great enthusiasm, but without financial support, to build up their settlement during the height of the Depression. Building materials were not to be readily available until the 1950s. The houses sitting on rocky outcrops were made from flattened kerosene tins. On the southern side of the site where there was some soil a few mud huts were constructed. The missionaries had more substantial houses made of stone. The community also built a church. Eaton made furniture for himself and showed others how to make it. However, people were still living in houses made of rusty kerosene tins in 1954.[10] Four years later there were complaints that the cottages were tumbling down

Nepabunna house under construction by Bill Stubbs, Ted Wilton, Walter Coulthard, Chris Ryan, Sam Coulthard and Fred Eaton.

[SAMA1083/23/4078, SAM]

House made from flattened kerosene tins with Sydney and Elsie Jackson and some of their children, c. 1934.

[SAMA1083/32/5879, SAM]

Lime mortar hut at Nepabunna, 1947.

[SAMA1083/42/8317, SAM]

A house at Nepabunna once lived in by the Wilton family with Mount
McKinlay in the distance.

[PRG1218/34/794C, Mountford Sheard Collection SLSA]

and there was serious overcrowding. Finally in 1959, eight new
cottages were built. But the housing continued to be inadequate
through the 1960s. The UAM did not have the financial resources
to increase or improve housing. The people complained that the
houses were totally inadequate for the extremes of cold and heat
experienced in the area; they had no verandahs and many had
no guttering; bathrooms and laundries were deficient; and basic
facilities such as cupboards and sinks were lacking. Even though
the Adnyamathanha paid rent their houses were not maintained.

Employment

Some Adnyamathanha believe the missionaries saved them from starvation during the Depression when rabbiting became a major source of work and food, with only a few men working in the pastoral industry.[11] But at other times work was readily available in the North Flinders Ranges, and people were fully employed until the 1970s when the pastoral industry became less labour-intensive and it ceased to be a major employer of Aboriginal people.

In the 1940s, 1950s, and 1960s stations employed most of the men and boys, many of whom began work in their early teens, at very low rates of pay. In 1940 Eaton had talks with the Australian Workers Union organiser[12] and they agreed that Aboriginal people should be paid wages equal to other workers. It was often the stations closest to the Mission which exploited Aboriginal labour most. In 1939 it was claimed stations further away paid award wages of £2–12.-6 ($5.20) per week and no keep, while stations closer to Nepabunna paid £1 ($2.00) to 35·shillings per week plus keep. [13] In 1950 the policeman at Farina claimed there were unscrupulous station managers who cheated the Aborigines by paying them on paper, but then taking all their wages by charging them exorbitant prices for clothes and food. He quoted the example of a man who had not received wages for months because of this situation.[14] However he noted that not all stations were exploitative. At Witchelina, where the officer negotiated a job for Jack Forbes ensuring he had a cottage and food for his family and was paid £7 per week, the manager, McCormick paid his stockmen equal wages.[15]

Employment was also available in mining. There were various mines dotted around the Flinders, for instance, silver, lead, copper and barytes mines and a talc mine at Mount Fitton. In 1940 Eaton arranged for the Adnyamathanha to mine silver and lead

Men and children with donkey team and wagon collecting firewood
at Wirrealpa station.

[SAMA1083/32/5975, SAM]

sixteen kilometres from Nepabunna, and in 1948 he established a
barytes mine not far from the Mission which continued operating
until 1957.. Ted Coulthard and a few other men established their
own mining claims from time to time, or in other ways were self-
employed. Ted Coulthard and his brother Dick, continued to
cart materials with their donkey teams, and Rufus Wilton had
a contract in 1942 erecting telephone posts. Women obtained
work as domestic servants at station homesteads or in nearby
townships such as Blinman and Copley.

The opening of the Leigh Creek coalfields in the 1940s created
a new opportunity for regular employment for the men. There
was work not only on the coalfields, but also on the roads and
railway associated with them. For several decades the Electricity
Trust of South Australia, which worked the coalfields and built

Donkey team pulling broken-down car at Nepabunna, late 1930s.
[PRG1218/34/834C, Mountford Sheard Collection SLSA]

Leigh Creek township, banned Aboriginal people from living there. Adnyamathanha employed at the mines or in associated industries were forced to camp at Copley or Beltana. The racist attitudes of many Electricity Trust employees ensured that Adnyamathanha would not have felt comfortable living in the Leigh Creek township even had they had the option of doing so.

Education
As a result of this history of full employment among the Adnyamathanha people, Nepabunna became the dormitory of the community. It was the place where people came to rest between

Sports meeting at Nepabunna, late 1930s.
[PRG1218/34/817B, SLSA Mountford Sheard Collection]

jobs, or when they were old or sick. It was a haven for women and children while the men were out working on stations, although many men took their families with them. The mobility of families, and more particularly the extremely erratic schooling which was available at Nepabunna resulted in children receiving only a very basic education. The missionaries, first the Eatons and then the Hathaways, were not trained teachers nor were they able to devote themselves to teaching as they had all the responsibilities of running the Mission. Most of the children at Nepabunna never progressed beyond the early years of primary school until the Education Department took over the school in the early 1960s.

Eaton built a dormitory on the Mission to enable parents to leave their children in school while they were away on stations, but it was rarely used. Some people moved away from the Mission so that their children could attend regular primary schools in towns such as Copley, Beltana, Blinman and Hawker. By the 1960s some moved to Port Augusta and other larger towns to ensure their children obtain a secondary school education. In the 1980s children were bussed into the Leigh Creek secondary school, a one and a half hour trip each way.

Diet

The move to Nepabunna probably did not have any immediate impact on the diet of the people. The old and sick were assured of rations distributed by the missionaries, and others bought food with the wages they earned, or were fed from the homesteads when they were working on the stations. They could always supplement their European diet with game and wild seeds and fruits which they collected. One woman who came to live at Nepabunna from Colebrook home and Point Pearce thought the rations she was issued inferior in variety to those she had received previously.[16] The rations which were distributed in 1945 were per adult per week: '7lb flour, 1lb sugar, 2oz tea, salt, tobacco, baking powder, oatmeal or rice, soap'.[17] Eaton suggested the old and sick needed this diet supplemented with milk, jam, dried fruit, vegetables and meat.[18] He did at one time grow vegetables himself to distribute to those on rations. Some Adnyamathanha grew their own fruit and vegetables. Ted Coulthard had a thriving garden with apple, orange, lemon, apricot and mulberry trees and grapes, strawberries and vegetables. He carted the water he needed from the well.[19]

Water

Nepabunna did not have an accessible water supply and this continued to be a problem until the 1970s. When the Mission was established, Eaton not only undertook a lot of the construction work himself, but sank wells looking for water. In 1944 he sank a well 34 metres deep without finding water.[20] Years later Hathaway claimed diviners had found water, but the Engineering and Water

Nepabunna, late 1947.
[SAMA1083/42/8319, SAM]

Supply Department disputed his claim as they had unsuccessfully drilled for water in the area.[21] In the 1960s the UAM did not have the resources to improve the water supply which was another reason why the Adnyamathanha wanted the government to take over the Mission.

Health and hygiene

The rocky Nepabunna site not only made it difficult to drill for water and build houses, but once the houses were constructed and the water supply ensured, it was still difficult to install a hygienic, modern effluent system. In 1945, a visiting policeman was horrified to find that there were twenty huts and houses at the Mission with no lavatories and that the people still used the creek beds for their effluent. He pointed out the health hazards and the fact that illnesses spread by flies, such as sore eyes and dysentery, were prevalent in the community.[22] William Penhall, the Protector of Aborigines, dismissed the police officer's concern claiming that in his experience supplying conveniences would not improve the situation as they would not be used.[23] By the late 1940s the houses had been fitted with Hygieno pans, which had to be emptied regularly. This work was left to the women as the men were frequently away. The women did not have the means to cart the effluent very far. Disposal of effluent in watershed areas close to residential areas was still a problem in 1967.[24]

Health care was another on-going problem for the Nepabunna community. By the time Nepabunna was established the Adnyamathanha were reliant on European forms of health care, but there was no trained health worker resident in the community. The women had their babies at home as late as the early 1960s assisted by Rebecca Forbes, a white woman married to Jack Forbes, an Adnyamathanha man. The missionaries kept a register of births. For other medical treatment the sick had to travel far afield. In the early days the journey from Nepabunna to Copley was quite arduous and slow, and Copley was only a stage on the way to the doctor at Hawker or the hospital at Port Augusta or Adelaide. Eaton tried to obtain a house in Copley in which people could stay on their way to seek medical attention,[25] but the sick continued to have to camp out in Copley while they waited for the train south. Eaton, who often sent outraged and outspoken letters to the Protector of Aborigines about continuing social inequities, pointed out in one such letter that 'his' people had to travel twelve hours by train past two hospitals which would not accept them before they could receive medical attention.[26] The only facilities for complex medical procedures and specialist attention were in Adelaide. The trip south away from family and friends was difficult and demanding for an old person who had never left country and might never return. The possibility of someone dying far from home was extremely disturbing for the community, as it has always been considered important for people to die and be buried in their own country.

The community at Nepabunna were dependent on the missionaries to arrange medical treatment and were sometimes blamed when people died. The missionaries controlled the transport to take the people into Copley, and the radio receiver, which the community had helped purchase, through which contact could be made with the Flying Doctor Service.

System of relief

The system of government relief available to Aboriginal people in South Australia, including the Adnyamathanha, was complex and inequitable. When Nepabunna was established distribution of rations was the only form of government support for Aboriginal people. During the Depression most of the people were dependent on rations distributed by the missionary Jim Page at Ram Paddock Gate, but by the 1940s when employment was available only the old and sick received rations. Stringent guidelines for the distribution of rations were issued, so that policemen and others issuing them were very concerned about justifying their actions and it became a legitimised way of harassing Aboriginal people. This is exemplified by the experience of a group of Adnyamathanha people who were passing through Beltana in 1939. They had been given a fortnight's supply of rations when they left Nepabunna over three weeks previously. They applied to the local policeman for supplies to enable them to return to Nepabunna. The policeman searched their camp to verify they had no food before issuing rations and then notified Mr Eaton he had done so, to ensure that they did not apply to him for the same rations.[27]

In 1955 the new policeman at Blinman, who had not issued

rations before, was sent the following guidelines by the Protector of Aborigines:

1. Full blood, uneducated Aborigines are to be considered as deserving special assistance and any requests for relief should be considered sympathetically.
2. Part Aborigines should as far as possible seek employment and provide for themselves and their families, always realising that certain native characteristics are likely to show up and their cases could therefore be viewed somewhat more sympathetically than ordinary Europeans. Relief should be issued to genuinely unemployed, sick, widowed and old. They should also be provided with medical attention and some form of shelter.[28]

By the 1940s women were receiving child endowment and maternity allowances. However, these were paid to the missionaries rather than directly to the mother. Under the South Australian *Aborigines Act* all people of Aboriginal descent were defined as Aborigines, but under federal legislation in the 1940s access to child endowment payments depended on the percentage of 'Aboriginal blood' of the mother. A 'halfcaste' woman was eligible for child endowment payments, but a mother with more than half 'Aboriginal blood' was defined as a 'fullblood' and not eligible.[29] The missionaries also had difficulty obtaining child endowment for many women at the Mission who had traditional marriages which were not recognised by the government. The births had to be registered under the mother's name only and were regarded by the authorities as illegitimate. There were many other anomalies in the system. For instance, an Aboriginal person of mixed descent living in the general community could apply for a widow's or old age pension. As soon as that person moved on to a mission, however, the pension was cancelled and the only relief available to them was rations.[30] Eaton pointed out to the Protector of Aborigines the inequity of a system which taxed Aborigines who worked, but refused to pay them a pension when they no longer were able to work.[31]

Aboriginal people could remove themselves from the vagaries of the Aboriginal relief system by applying for exemption from the *Aborigines Act*. This meant they were no longer officially regarded as an Aborigine; they could no longer enter Aboriginal Reserves, or apply for rations, but could have access to alcoholic liquor and receive pensions on the same basis as the general population. The exemption system had its own anomalies. The Protector of Aborigines could cancel a person's exemption, so Aboriginal people were not entirely free of the Aborigines Protection Board. Exemptions often applied to individuals rather than to families, so an exempted person might be married to an unexempted spouse. Within this family situation it would be illegal for one marriage partner to supply the other with liquor. It also split extended families in other ways. An exempted person such as Rufus Wilton could not visit his family and friends at Nepabunna. On the other hand he was free to send his children to whatever school he chose without interference from the missionaries or the Aborigines Protection Board.

The missionaries

Over the 43 years that Nepabunna operated as a Mission there were three missionaries in charge. Jim Page first arrived at Ram Paddock Gate in the late 1920s and was soon joined by Fred Eaton. Jim Page died in 1935 and Fred Eaton and his wife retired in the early 1950s. Bill and Florence Hathaway settled at Nepabunna in 1954 and stayed there until 1973 when the South Australian

Christmas at Nepabunna, late 1930s.
[PGR1218/34/724H Mountford Sheard Collection SLSA]

government took over the settlement. The Hathaways then moved to Copley. The UAM still served Nepabunna from Copley in the 1980s through an Adnyamathanha minister Willie Austin.

The missionaries were responsible for running the settlement. The Adnyamathanha had no control over their community. All government payments made to Aborigines were made through the missionaries. They gave out rations, ran the store, were responsible for the water supply, regulated admission to the settlement, provided medical care in minor cases and arranged transport to doctor or hospital in more serious cases, and ran and taught at the school. But they regarded these responsibilities as secondary to their primary task of converting Aboriginal people to Christianity.

Living conditions in Copley

Adnyamathanha people not only lived on stations, and at Nepabunna, but also in the towns dotted through the Flinders Ranges such as Copley, Beltana, Blinman and Hawker. By the mid-1940s there were a number of families living in Copley and Beltana who were attracted by employment available in industries associated with the Leigh Creek coalfields. As they could not obtain housing in Leigh Creek, they set up camps in Copley. Some tried to buy houses or land in the town, but financial support from the Aborigines Department was not forthcoming. The local non-Aboriginal population did not want Adnyamathanha camping in the middle of the township, and they were harassed

Copley to Nepabunna track, late 1930s.
[PRG1218/34/728E SLSA]

by the local policeman. Walter and Andy Coulthard made a number of submissions to the Protector of Aborigines asking him to intervene on their behalf so they could settle somewhere permanently. They had been forced to send their families back to Nepabunna, interrupting their children's education at Copley Primary School, and had their furniture piled up on Copley Common. Eventually in 1948 permission was granted for three families, those of Andy and Walter Coulthard and Maurice Johnson, to camp on the Copley Common Reserve northeast of the town.[32] This permission did not extend to other people camping for periods of more than forty eight hours in Copley. The Reserve had no water supply and they had to pay 3 shillings per 455 litres to have the water carted, costing them up to 9 shillings per week. The carter was unreliable and they often had to carry a bucket at least a kilometre to get drinking water.[33] Water was not made available to the campsite until August 1951.

Survival of traditional life

When the Adnyamathanha settled at Nepabunna they retained many aspects of their traditional life. The economic basis of traditional life had been undermined by the advent of the colonists and the pastoral and mining industries, but they had adapted to the new money economy and European forms of employment. Traditional attitudes, beliefs and ceremonies associated with birth, marriage, death and relationships among families and relatives still survived. The Adnyamathanha people today often refer to these traditional controls as the 'rules'. Life on the Mission gradually undermined these controls so by the time the missionaries moved away from Nepabunna in 1973 European controls and laws prevailed, although many traditional attitudes and beliefs persist.

The major time of crisis for the Adnyamathanha people in resolving the conflicts of the two systems of social control under which they lived came in the mid and late 1940s. Conduct which broke the strict rules of traditional law was no longer dealt with in a traditional manner, because that in turn would have broken European law. For instance, certain sexual misconduct was punished traditionally by the death of the offender. Such conduct in the mid-1940s was dealt with in a milder, 'legal' way according to European law, involving social ostracism but not death.[34]

In the late 1940s there was also a series of crises related to the survival of initiation ceremonies. The last initiation ceremony was held in 1948, but prior to that some families had made independent decisions not to have their sons initiated which created tensions in the community when these uninitiated men wanted to marry. Finally in 1947–48 the pressures of living under two different systems of social and legal control seem to have been too great for the community and a decision was taken not to hold further initiations. The end of the initiation ceremonies heralded the end of other 'rules'. The last traditional marriages were performed in the early 1950s and people were no longer buried at separate gravesites according to moiety.

Some of the people blame the missionaries for the end of the 'rules',[35] others say it was a choice taken by the Adnyamathanha.[36] The missionaries established an environment at Nepabunna which made it increasingly difficult for the traditional forms of social control to survive. They allowed traditional rules to continue, although they did actively try to stop the final stage of *wilyaru* initiation, the second stage of the two stage initiation ceremony, involving mutilation of the back, but propagated a conflicting set of Christian beliefs the preaching of which they saw as their chief occupation.[37] Eaton articulated his hostility to

Nepabunna church, late 1930s.

[SAMA1083/32/5909, SAM]

the initiation ceremonies on religious grounds to the Protector of Aborigines.[38] He also did not welcome visits of the anthropologist, C.P. Mountford, who encouraged the performance of traditional ceremonies.[39]

The women at Nepabunna were more receptive to Eaton's evangelising than the men and this created pressures in the community over the continuation of the 'rules'. The Protector of Aborigines believed 'native rites' should not be prohibited as they would eventually die out and Aboriginal elders would lose control over their people. He would only intervene if young men were being initiated against their will.[40]

Other factors also contributed to the decision to stop initiations. The pastoral industry had deprived much of the country of its natural vegetation, which affected the performance of the ceremonies,[41] and the demands of the money economy

Fred McKenzie, late 1930s.
[PRG1218/34/726R Mountford Sheard Collection SLSA]

made it more difficult for people to come together in large gatherings. Another problem was the growing impact of the consumption of alcohol on the community.

These various influences made it more difficult for the men to go through the arduous ceremonies with the same conviction that their fathers had. As a result of these conflicting pressures Fred McKenzie, who was responsible for the ceremonies, and some of the elders decided to discontinue initiations.[39] There are many people in the Adnyamathanha community who regret the end of the 'rules' and would like to see the old traditions revived in a modified form.

Aspects of traditional life which have survived pressure from missionaries and European lifestyle are the Adnyamathanha language, social controls relating to intermarriage within the Adnyamathanha community, the moiety and naming system, and much of the mythology associated with traditional Adnyamathanha life. Many of the traditional attitudes also survive, such as attitudes to death and burial and to traditional Aboriginal sites.

5

1973–2018
Self-determination and
Native Title

In 1973 the South Australian government took over responsibility for Nepabunna from the United Aborigines Mission allowing the Adnyamathanha much more autonomy than they had experienced in many decades. In a short period of time the community had to learn to deal with a large variety of government departments and funding bodies both at the state and federal level. They had to develop an organisational basis on which to run their community which included people who had moved temporarily or semi-permanently to pastoral stations and towns as far afield as Port Augusta but still considered Nepabunna their home.

Although the Adnyamathanha no longer live on their lands as they did 160 years ago they continue to take the custodianship of the land very seriously. From the 1970s until the 1990s several Adnyamathanha worked for the Aboriginal Heritage Branch of the Department of Environment and Planning recording the location of mythological, historic, sacred and other sites which are important to their people.[1] Another four were employed by the National Parks and Wildlife Service as rangers. The Adnyamathanha have encouraged the general public to take an interest in their land by acting as guides to groups of school children and others interested in the Flinders Ranges and Adnyamathanha history and culture. In 1994 the Coulthard family established Iga Warta as a base for education and cultural tourism. It is used both to give Adnyamathanha children, many of whom live in towns, a cultural education as well as teaching local and international tourists about traditional Adnyamathanha rock art sites, mythology and religious life, art, culture and food.

Yura Ngawarla

Although the majority of Adnyamathanha no longer speak their language, Yura Ngawarla, at home, the community has worked hard to maintain the language and to pass it on from generation to generation. In the mid-1960s Andrew Coulthard worked with the linguist Bernard Schebeck recording traditional stories, and Schebeck produced the first grammar and phonology of the language.[2] In the late 1970s and 1980s another linguist, Dorothy Tunbridge, worked with community members, particularly Annie Coulthard, developing an orthography and recording traditional stories which were published as *Flinders Ranges Dreaming*.[3] At the same time Pearl and John McKenzie collaborated with one of the local pastoralists, John McEntee, producing Yura Ngawarla word lists and a dictionary published in 1992 based on a different orthography from that developed by Tunbridge. Their daughter Pauline now teaches the language at the Hawker Area School. More recently there have been various projects to maintain and teach the language at Nepabunna, Port Augusta and as far away as Adelaide where Adnyamathanha now reside. Several Adnyamathanha have published stories in their language, including Lily Neville whose handwritten and illustrated texts were published by Australians Against Racism in 2007.[4] In Adelaide Gillian Bovorro and others through their organisation

Inhaadi Adnyamathanha Ngawarla ensure the language is maintained far from their home country by running evening language classes, producing teaching materials and even making an animated film, *Wadu Matyidi*, about children encountering white men for the first time in the Flinders Ranges. Yura Ngawarla is taught in primary schools in the Flinders Ranges and the Port Augusta area as well as some preschools and high schools in the region.[5]

In 1985 Pearl McKenzie and Christine Davis published the *Adnyamathanha Genealogy*.[6] Relying on Pearl's detailed knowledge of family relationships and extensive consultation with Adnyamathanha families they showed how the various families in the community are descended from seven main family groups giving the community a detailed history of their family connections. The seven lines traced by the genealogists with their moiety associations are: Frome Charlie and wife Lucy Darmody, Mount Serle Bob and Polly, Willie Austin and Effie, Nicholas Demell and Emily McKenzie, Sydney Ryan and Mary, Angepena Billy and Fanny, and Jack Clarke and Sarah Johnson. The Adnyamathanha Traditional Lands Association (ATLA) is updating and digitising this genealogy for future generations.

Native title

A major concern of the Adnyamathanha as with all colonised Indigenous peoples is regaining control of their lands. In the 1970s and 1980s they gained some rights over two pastoral leases, Nantawarrina and Mount Serle and since then they have consolidated access to land across the region greatly facilitated by the *Native Title Act*. Native title has not only recognised their rights to land but has enabled them to negotiate with mining companies for royalties which have been distributed to the Adnyamathanha community in various ways as detailed below. The *Native Title Act, 1993* was passed by the federal parliament following the decision by the High Court in 1992 to recognise native title in the Torres Strait and by extension on the Australian mainland in *Mabo v Queensland* case. The Court held that Indigenous people in Australia held common law native title rights at the time of European settlement which continued to exist where they had not been extinguished by legislation or other executive acts of government.[7]

Soon after the Act was passed several Adnyamathanha put in individual or family-based native title claims, but it became clear that it would take many years to resolve these small and sometimes overlapping claims as has been the case in other regions of Australia. In some communities where family-based, rather than community-based claims have been submitted to the Native Title Tribunal, intra-community tensions have resulted which have become acrimonious, so rather than native title empowering these communities it has pulled them apart. The Adnyamathanha decided to consolidate their claims as one people and in 1998 submitted their claim across the north Flinders Ranges. In 2001 the Adnyamathanha Traditional Lands Association (ATLA) was established which became a Prescribed Body Corporate under regulations under the *Native Title Act* following their native title determinations. ATLA has a large governing committee (23 directors in 2018) with directors representing families, cultural and administrative groups. While there are still tensions and occasional conflicts between the various groups represented on the governing committee, the Adnyamathanha have recognised that their best interests are served by working together.

They received three consent determinations under the

Native Title Act from Justice John Mansfield of the Federal Court in 2009. These covered the pastoral lease Angepena station, a larger region of the north Flinders Ranges stretching from Lake Frome almost to the NSW border including Nepabunna and Mt Serle pastoral lease, and the Flinders Ranges National Park. The rights that these determinations granted varied depending on the colonial history of these lands. In a few areas the Adnyamathanha gained exclusive rights over the land, for instance Nepabunna and Mt Serle which they had previously claimed through the South Australian Aboriginal Lands Trust, in other areas they have rights to live on the land, hunt and gather food, hold ceremonies, bury their dead and maintain traditional practices, but share the land with other interested parties including the state.[8]

Since 2009 there have been further consent determinations over Adnyamathanha land. As of 2018 they have native title rights over approximately 70,000 sq kilometres of land with a few claims still outstanding.[9] They also have a number of Indigenous Land Use Agreements (ILUAs) and co-manage the Ikara-Flinders Ranges and Vulkathunha-Gammon Ranges National Parks. The management boards of these national parks have equal Adnyamathanha and government representation. The Adnyamathanha have negotiated permission to hunt over declared parts of the Vulkathunha national park, and in concert with National Parks and Wildlife have stopped proposed mining in the park. Although native title does not give the Adnyamathanha veto power over mining outside parks it does enable them to negotiate royalty agreements with mining companies. ATLA has set up Rangelea Holdings to accept and distribute royalty payments from the Beverley Uranium mine. These royalties are distributed twice a year to the Adnyamathanha and are also used to provide funds for funerals, support sporting events and promote health and education within the community.[10] ATLA established another company, Cramond Pty Ltd, to purchase the Wilpena Pound Resort in 2012 in partnership with Indigenous Business Australia. This flourishing business creates employment for Adnyamathanha people in management, hospitality and tourism. The Flinders Ranges have always attracted large numbers of tourists and the Adnyamathanha have now established a number of enterprises to service the industry, including, Iga Warta Tourism Operations, Nepabunna Cultural Tours and Four Winds Cultural Guiding.[11]

Native title has not only given the community access and some control over much of their lands but it has also given them the ability to assert their cultural rights, put resources into maintaining their language, created employment for their young people and a means of retaining their culture. ATLA and other individuals and organisations run programs where their children, many of whom now live in towns, learn about country and how it maintained and continues to nurture their people. These children are growing up in a very different world from their parents and grandparents.

Challenges in the twenty-first century

While native title has greatly empowered the Adnyamathanha, they still find themselves fighting to control new developments on their lands that have the potential either to pollute the country and/or to destroy sites of significance. In 2018 there are two major developments over which the community have grave concerns: a nuclear waste dump proposed for Wallerberdina station near Hawker; and coal gasification at Leigh Creek coalfields.

Proposals from both the federal and state governments have identified the Flinders Ranges as a site for low and medium level nuclear waste. While the leaseholder of Wallerberdina strongly supports some of his land being used as a storage facility, most of the Adnyamathanha and many other local residents, including neighbouring landholders are strongly opposed. ATLA among other organisations is lobbying to have the proposal overturned.

Mining at the Leigh Creek coalfields was discontinued by Alinta Energy in 2015 when the company closed the Port Augusta power station which was the sole user of the low grade coal. The mining site is now being remediated and the township which provided accommodation for mine workers has been handed back to the state government that built it in 1982. A report was released in June 2016 which considered the future options for the township as it moved from a closed company town to an open town supporting local businesses and economic opportunities.[12] While the Adnyamathanha were mentioned as a group to be consulted, the report does not give any indication of what their interests in the future of the town might be. Up until the 1980s Leigh Creek and its predecessor were closed company towns. As mentioned previously they did not provide accommodation for Aboriginal people, even those employed in the mines or associated industries, so they were forced into makeshift accommodation in Copley and Beltana. The first Adnyamathanha family to live in Leigh Creek in the 1980s were the late Don Coulthard, his wife Sissi and their children. The Adnyamathanha through ATLA are negotiating with the government to allow more families to access housing in the town. As of 2018 there were 11 Adnyamathanha families resident in Leigh Creek.

The Leigh Creek coalfields sit on an important site associated with one of the Adnyamathanha creation ancestors, Yurlu the Kingfisher stopped there on his way to a ceremony and built a fire to send a smoke signal he was on his way. The remnants of his fire formed the coal which has been commercially mined since 1943. The community does not want the defunct coalmines merely scientifically remediated as proposed by the government, but they want to repair the damage to one of their traditional sites. This aspiration has been undermined by plans of Leigh Creek Energy Ltd to trial underground coal gasification which would not only further damage a traditional site, but could cause widespread pollution. It is a technology that has been banned in many parts of the world, including in Queensland. In September 2018 the Adnyamathanha lost a bid in the Supreme Court to stop this underground gas extraction.[13]

Many, although not all Adnyamathanha, have also been fighting to have the Beverley and Four Mile uranium mines closed. Uranium has been mined there since the beginning of the century by pumping acid into an aquifer which dissolves the uranium ore and other heavy metals. It is then pumped to the surface and the uranium extracted and the radioactive waste dumped polluting the ground water for many years to come. Native title rights have not given the title holders the capacity to stop mining to which they object.

This century has also presented opportunities for the Adnyamathanha. Their children can now access all levels of education. In 2010 Rebecca Richards became the first Aboriginal person to gain a Rhodes Scholarship to Oxford University. She is now completing a PhD in anthropology while working at the South Australian Museum. Other Adnyamathanha have continued to be involved in researching and preserving the heritage of their people. Cliff Coulthard facilitated the archaeological research into an ancient site on Adnyamathanha land at Warratyi rock shelter having previously undertaken research into rock art in the Lascaux caves in France. Warratyi presents evidence that humans occupied the arid interior of Australia at least 49,000 years ago cohabiting with the now extinct megafauna such as the *Diptrotodon optatum*. The site also presents evidence of the earliest use of ochre in Australia and Southeast Asia, as well as bone tools, hafted tools and stone artefacts.[14]

Recognition of Adnyamathanha sovereignty

Since the mid-1980s the Adnyamathanha have been developing their own flag which represents the sky, the people, the land, men's and women's story lines, Ikara (Wilpena Pound) and ATLA governing body.[15] At the same time the Adnyamathanha have been working to gain recognition as a autonomous people. At

Celebrations for Nepabunna's 80th anniversary in 2011,
with the Adnyamathanha flag in the background.
[Photo Peggy Brock]

Celebrations for Nepabunna's 80th anniversary in 2011.
[Photos by Peggy Brock]

the end of 2016 the government announced it would commence discussions over the possibility of a series of treaties with Aboriginal communities in South Australia. Dr Roger Thomas, a Kokatha/Mirning man was appointed Treaty Commissioner and in August 2017 Aboriginal communities were invited to submit applications. Three communities, including the Adnyamathanha, were subsequently invited to participate in a treaty-making process.[16] With a change of government in March 2018 treaty negotiations were discontinued, to be replaced by discussions across a broad range of issues affecting Aboriginal people in which ATLA is still recognised by the government as the Adnyamathanha representative body in negotiations.

This history of the late twentieth and early twenty-first century reflects the changes that have occurred in the lives of Aboriginal people in South Australia. Up until 1973 the Adnyamathanha had limited autonomy. If they lived at Nepabunna they had to conform to the discipline and authority of the missionaries. If they lived away from the mission, they often found themselves segregated from other local residents in towns. Over the past 40 years they have taken control of their own communities. They are free to live where they choose, they have gained access and some control of their lands and have learned to operate effectively in the money economy, negotiate with companies and government, build up their own businesses, and access all levels of education. One man who epitomises these changes over half a century is Vince Coulthard, who, like so many Adnyamathanha born in the 1950s lived at Nepabunna mission, worked in the Flinders Ranges on pastoral properties and elsewhere before taking up government employment and then becoming a spokesman and community leader. He tells this history from his own lived experience.

Vince Coulthard. [Photo Dave Haslett]

Vince Coulthard[17]

My Dad, Clem, was born at Wooltana before they moved to Nepabunna. My Mum, Lena, was born at Nepabunna. My mother's parents Walter and Helen Coulthard they got married at Bolla Bollana. There were old smelters there and grandfather worked round the area pretty well up in that Mt Fitton Arkaroola area. Building fences doing all kinds of things. My paternal grandparents, Ted Coulthard and Winnie Ryan, they lived at Minara Vutu that is Ram Paddock. Grandfather had got the contract for the old telegraph line from Wooltana to Balcanoona. He also carted wool and fencing material to a lot of the station properties from Beltana in those days. They said wait til the wool's actually paid. No you don't need to pay me but I want some land for my stock. There was a gentleman's handshake for the place that is now known as Iga Warta area. One of the things my grandfather had to do then was fence that area off. That's history. Missionaries came along and that's how Jim Page moved across to Nepabunna with the community from Ram Paddock. They went to White Well where Iga Warta is now and they went to sink a well but the water was too deep so they moved to Nepabunna, rightfully so it should have been grandfather's land. That's his payment for carting wool and fencing material for the pastoralists.

That's where I grew up, Nepabuuna. I went to school there. I went there the second year after the Education Department took over the school. I did all my primary school there. Came down to Port Augusta in the early '70s. I did one year down there and didn't like Port Augusta, didn't like the school. It was a bit of a culture shock because I went to school where there were all Aboriginal kids, a couple of white kids but we were the majority. In Port Augusta I just stood in the corner. I was just so afraid of all these kids. It was a bit of a scary ordeal actually and I went back to Mum and Dad and said I didn't want to go back to school and Dad said OK if you don't want to go to school you find a job and you do it by yourself. So I went up to Arkaroola. Dad was working up at Arkaroola at the time. He was building roads there for the ridgetop tour and running tours. I went to see the old chef there. He said there's a big bag of spuds there you can start peeling them. That was my first job peeling spuds and washing dishes and all these pots and pans. It wasn't really what I wanted to do. We were driving one weekend back to Nepabunna and we stopped in at Balcanoona. I started the following week as a station hand. That's what I really wanted to do. I loved riding horses. As kids we went to Balcanoona we helped with mustering. Dad really wanted the others to get an education so he and Mum made the decision to move to Port Augusta. On Friday he got a job with the railways and on Monday he started. He got a house in Port Augusta and moved Mum down. I was 15 then. Dad stayed on until he retired. Later I followed my brother Terence to the Gawler Ranges and worked there for a short time.

Then I came back and worked for the city council Port Augusta. I worked on the road gang packing dirt, rolling the bitumen. It wasn't a really good job. Most of the work is done in summer and the heat off the road as well as the smell is horrible. Then I went back bush a very short time to Nepabunna when they were doing up the houses there. Then I was working at the preschool, Tji tji wiltja, driving the bus picking kids up, and my grandfather, Walter, wanted me to take notes at a meeting. So I went along. It's that time that probably changed my life when I started attending meetings. I was shadowing him. I used to spend a lot of time with him meeting politicians and so on in the '70s. He was a good friend of Don Dunstan's so there'd be times when I'd bring him down to Adelaide and I'd take him round to Don's place and I thought who is this Don. One day in Port Augusta Don Dunstan came up to give a speech in Gladstone Square. And when Dunstan came off the rotunda he was talking to grandfather. And I said what is he? He's a government man. He's the big boss of the government.

He discussed a lot of land issues with Dunstan and rights. He had been meeting with Don since the '60s. I didn't understand politics in the '60s. I was only young myself. We were out at Nepabunna and we'd go out riding donkeys and go bush. We had better things to do than worry about rights. I didn't understand much about politics until the '70s when grandfather got me involved with these meetings.

I worked for National Parks for 12 years. I did a year in 1980 and then they decided to take on 4 trainees and we had more formal training. I initially started at Oraparinna, then went to Balcanoona and Vulkathunha National Park, then they retrenched me back to Wilpena, then I came to Port Augusta for a while to manage the Aboriginal Programs Unit [of SA

National Parks]. Then there was a change in government and Aboriginal Heritage was put in Aboriginal Affairs. The problem with Aboriginal Affairs is it just deals with policy and doesn't police sites. Prior to that the National Parks rangers would inspect Aboriginal heritage sites and we could prosecute. We did a report on BHP for site damage at Iron Baron. That caused a real turmoil in government it stopped all the works there. Because it was BHP a big company the government wanted to look after them. Hey! No different from the fights we're having today with the nuclear waste dump and Leigh Creek. Big companies they don't care about our sites. It's unbelievable, the same old fight. The government doesn't care about preserving Aboriginal sites, that's what I said to the minister at a meeting. The same as my grandfather said 40 or 50 years ago how important it is to preserve our culture and our sites, our story lines. We're lucky, the Adnyamathanha people, because we live in the oldest mountain range in the world, Flinders. Aboriginal people, we're the oldest living culture and this is something Australia hasn't come to terms with yet. We have sites that are thousands and thousands of years old. Cliff [Coulthard] was recently involved in the Warratyi excavation where they found where Aboriginal people were eating the megafauna. It changes the history of human occupation in the time of the megafauna.

I worked for National Parks till the early '90s when I took a package. At the same time they were building an Aboriginal radio station at Port August and they asked me to go help them set it up and manage it. I set it up out of a caravan. And I thought this is alright, I can handle this radio. It was funded by the Commonwealth with support from ABC radio with programs. So I applied and was successful. I'm still there today doing part time radio Umeewarra 8.9 FM community radio in Port Augusta. The feds cut funding and we're down to 4 staff now broadcasting 24/7 we do that with 2 broadcast staff and volunteers. The whole idea of the radio station is to bring the community to the radio.

When I went to work for Umeewarra the Mabo [native title] case was starting. The first claim was put in by Gordon Coulthard for Wooltana and Balcanoona he looked at those 2 properties. And then we had another in Beltana/Leigh Creek area by Beverley and Stewart Patterson on the other side we had Angelina [Stuart] put in a claim, Geraldine [Anderson] put in a claim, everybody putting in small claims. It became difficult to keep up with it. I said wouldn't it be better to put it all in one claim. It took till 1996 to put our report together and get everybody into agreement. It wasn't till 1998 that we had the claim registered. Eleven years later we were successful in our determination in 2009. It was a hard task. Just took perseverance, negotiating with people.

ATLA has done a lot of good work, not just native title, pulling together the people, running programs, utilizing the negotiated funds from one company to run programs for the community. Sporting events for young people, it sponsors teams in the state carnival, it supports our people to elite sporting events. Cultural events, women's camp, language reclamation. Getting kids out on to country, also teaching them our cultural ways showing kids survival skills. Bush camps to Sacred Canyon talking about men's issues. Little Adnyamathanha kids they've grown up in town. It is about them learning. Sitting round talking to these old blokes getting them to talk about history and language and kinship, the father–son relationship and boy and uncle relationship, and respect and use appropriate language and be mindful to your relationship to the people around you and the way you talk.

Teaching all that to these kids. Most live in Port Augusta, a lot moving back to Leigh Creek. We got 11 families back there. The biggest number of Aboriginal people in history living in Leigh Creek now.

The highlight of our society today for Aboriginal people certainly Adnyamathanha is native title. It doesn't give us everything we want it's the best we can get today. What would be certainly the ultimate would be to get a treaty or some agreement like a treaty. But native title gives a right to a seat at the table and to negotiate. Our biggest achievement would be developing ATLA. In my view it is one of the best things that's happened in my lifetime since white man come here I guess.

We want something culturally appropriate the directors are based on families and interest groups like language. First we have elder male and elder female directors. We have core family groups and interest groups like language groups like Aroona council and Copley or Nepabunna Council and Iga Warta nominate a rep, and then there's those others who don't come from those sort of communities they have family groups to represent their interests. It works really well. People will have all kinds of opinion but you can't please everybody. I think we did damn well with this developing ATLA.

When we negotiate with mining companies for compensation and royalties we put them in a trust which is invested in Wilpena Resort and other property but also there are royalties we give to another company which distributes them. We're getting smart about doing business we set up a company to look after the business, a company to look after investment and a company to distribute the money. People have to register with date of birth and who they are related to. We want to continue the genealogy that Christine Davis [and Pearl McKenzie] put together and want to digitise it. There's also the funeral fund. That's something that's well received.

There's a lot more we could do if got some government support. We do this with our money. Its money we negotiated from mining. We can say we built this ourselves without government support. Native title doesn't give a veto of mining but we have the right to negotiate and any future act they've got to come to us and talk to us and get our endorsement.

Notes

Introduction

1   Capt. Charles Sturt, *Two Expeditions into the Interior of Southern Australia During the Years 1828, 1829, 1830, 1831: with observations on the soil, climate and general resources of the Colony of New South Wales*, vol. 2, ebooks@Adelaide, 2010, chapters 5, 6 and 7.

2   Peter Dowling, 'Violent Epidemics: Disease, conflict and Aboriginal population collapse as a result of European contact in the Riverland of South Australia' MA thesis, ANU, Canberra, 1990, suggests syphilis probably was transmitted from the coast introduced by whalers and sealers, while smallpox spread along the River Murray from the east coast pp. 101, 107–111; Steven Hemmings, 'Conflict Between Aborigines and Europeans along the Murray River from the Darling to the Great South Bend (1830–41)' Honours Thesis, Department of History, Adelaide, 1982, p. 16.

3   Christine Lockwood, 'Early Encounters on the Adelaide Plains and Encounter Bay' in Peggy Brock and Tom Gara, *Colonialism and Its Aftermath: A history of Aboriginal South Australia*, Adelaide: Wakefield Press, 2017, 68

4   Robert Foster, 'Feasts of the Full-Moon: the distribution of rations to Aborigines in South Australia, 1836–1861', *Aboriginal History* 13 (13 (1), 1989, 63–78.

The Adnyamathanha

1   Rufus Wilton, personal communication.

2   Luise A. Hercus and Isobel M. White, 'Perception of Kinship Structure Reflected in the Adnjamathanha Pronouns' in *Papers in Australian Linguistics* No. 6, Canberra, 1973, p. 50. C.P. Mountford, fieldnotes Vol. 20, Mountford-Sheard collection, State Library of South Australia.

3   Adnyamathanha initiations were held in two stages, *wilyaru* initiation being the second stage.
4   The Wangkangurru [Wonguranda] man later married an Adnyamathanha woman. Rufus Wilton, personal communication.
5   Rufus Wilton, personal communication.
6   Claude Demell, personal communication.
7   See below for discussion of moiety.
8   R. Ellis, 'The Funeral Beliefs of the Adnjamathanha' in *Journal of the Anthropological Society of South Australia*, Vol. 13, No. 6, 1975, p. 3.
9   B. Schebeck, 'The Atynymatana Personal Pronoun and the Wailpi Kinship System' in *Papers in Australian Linguistics* No. 6, Canberra, 1973, p. 25.
10 R. Ellis, 'Aboriginal Man in the Ranges' in *The Future of the Flinders Ranges*, Proceedings of a Seminar, Department of Adult Education, Adelaide, 1972, p. 5.

1840-1870 The Establishment of Colonial Settlement

1   Rufus Wilton, personal communication.
2   Bill Stubbs, personal communication.
3   J.F. Hayward, Diary 1846–56 in Royal Geographical Society of Australia, South Australian Branch, Vol. 29, 1927–28.
4   Ibid. p. 107.
5   John Bowyer Bull, Reminiscences 1835–94, PRG 507/3, State Library of South Australia.
6   Ibid.
7   Ibid.
8   Hayward, p. 98.
9   *Pastoral Pioneers of South Australia*, Vol. 1, Adelaide, 1974, p. 81b.
10 Bull, Reminiscences.
11 GRG/24/6/3481,3513,3546, State Records of South Australia.
12 Bull, Reminiscences. This account is probably essentially accurate, but Bull has exaggerated the details of Puttapa Bob's arrest.
13 Ibid.
14 GRG/5/2/593/172, State Records of South Australia.
15 GRG/5/2/776/57, State Records of South Australia.
16 GRG/5/2/593/1857, State Records of South Australia.
17 GRG/5/2/776/1857, State Records of South Australia.
18 John McKenzie, personal communication.
19 GRG/5/2/593/1857, State Records of South Australia.
20 GRG/5/2/130/1858 State Records of South Australia.
21 GRG/5/2/662/1858, State Records of South Australia.
22 GRG/5/2/514/1858, State Records of South Australia.
23 Ibid.
24 Ibid.

25 SA Parliamentary Papers 1865 No. 24.

26 *South Australian Register* 12/7/1865.

27 For instance, the measles epidemic of 1902 at Mount Serle which killed eight adults. See p. 35.

28 GRG/52/1/29/9/66,29/12/66,25/1/70, State Records of South Australia. Epidemics and illness among the Adnyamathanha have not been well documented.

29 Philip Jones, *Ochre and Rust: Artefacts and encounters on Australian frontiers,* Adelaide: Wakefield Press, 2007, 348–49

30 Rufus Wilton, personal communication.

31 Rufus Wilton, personal communication.

32 John McKenzie and Rufus Wilton, personal communication. Larrikin Tom died at Nepabunna as a very old man in 1936.

33 GRG/5/2/1863/6/12/63, State Records of South Australia.

34 SA Archives GRG/5/2/PCO 21/12/1863. Other places and people mentioned in the report are Mannuwolkininna, Mendonada and the so-called copper mine tribes.

35 See Jones, *Ochre and Rust,* 351–3.

36 SA Archives GRG/5/2/1864/4/1/1864.

37 *Port Augusta Dispatch* 9/6/1882.

38 GRG/5/2/1864/15/1/1864, State Records of South Australia.

39 Possibly George Noble of Balcanoona Station.

40 John McKenzie, personal communication.

41 Rufus Wilton suggests he was a Jadliaura man.

42 A.W. Howitt, *Native Tribes of Southeast Australia*, London, 1904, p. 47.

43 SA Archives GRG/5/2/1864 1217/1864, State Records of South Australia.

44 GRG/52/1/1/10/1869, State Records of South Australia.

45 GRG/52/1/14/11/70, State Records of South Australia.

46 Jones, *Ochre and Rust*, 370–71

47 SA Museum Archives Accession No. 162 26/12/1904.

48 GRG/52/1/265/1904.315/1904, State Records of South Australia.

49 GRG/53/1/40/1905, State Records of South Australia. See also Jones, *Ochre and Rust*, 273–74.

1870-1920s The Adnyamathanha and the Pastoral Economy

1 *Yura Newsletter*, Aboriginal Heritage Section, Vol. I. No. 4, 1977 p. 4. Story told by Wally Coulthard.

2 *Yura Newsletter*, Aboriginal Heritage Section, Vol. 1. No. 7, 1978, p. 9.

3 GRG/5/300 Vol. 2,6/6/1901, 1/1/1910, State Records of South Australia.

4 GRG/52/1/93/1893, State Records of South Australia.

5 Ibid.

6 GRG/52/1/1/1903, State Records of South Australia.

7   GRG/5/300/7, 15/9/1894, 6/11/1896, 8/8/1897, 2/11/1898, State Records of
    South Australia.
8   GRG/52/1/406/1894, State Records of South Australia.
9   GRG/52/1/375/1888, 190/1895, State Records of South Australia.
10 GRG/52/1/378/1897, State Records of South Australia.
11 GRG/52/1/5/2/1898, State Records of South Australia.
12 *South Australian Register* 27/3/1897.
13 GRG/52/1/329/1897, State Records of South Australia.
14 Ibid.
15 Ibid.
16 GRG52/1/190/1895, State Records of South Australia.

1931-73 Nepabunna Mission

1   Betty Ross, *Minerawuta (Ram Paddock Gate)*, Adelaide: Heritage Unit, SA
    Department for the Environment, 1981, 6.
2   Ross, *Minerawuta (Ram Paddock Gate)*, 4.
3   John McKenzie, personal communication.
4   *Yura Muda-Yura Tarta Yura Treaty*, Port Augusta: ATLA 13.
5   GRG/52/1/1930, State Records of South Australia.
6   GRG/52/1/1933, State Records of South Australia.
7   Rufus Wilton, personal communication.
8   C.P. Mountford, fieldnotes, Vol. 20, 1938 Mountford-Sheard collection, State
    Library of South Australia.
9   GRG/52/1/1159/66, State Records of South Australia.
10 GRG/52/1/14/6/54, State Records of South Australia.
11 Rufus Wilton, personal communication.
12 GRG/52/1/2//8/40, State Records of South Australia.
13 GRG/52/1/3/6/39, State Records of South Australia.
14 GRG/52/1/22/6/50, State Records of South Australia.
15 Ibid.
16 GRG/52/1114/8/49, State Records of South Australia.
17 GRG/52/1/22/2/45, State Records of South Australia.
18 Ibid.
19 Clem Coulthard, personal communication.
20 GRG/52/1/18/3/44, State Records of South Australia.
21 GRG/52/1/27/12/45, State Records of South Australia.
22 Ibid.
23 Ibid.
24 GRG/52/1/1599/66, State Records of South Australia.
27 GRG/52/1/20/4/46, State Records of South Australia.
26 GRG/52/1/17/2/50, State Records of South Australia.
27 GRG/52/1/11/10/39, State Records of South Australia.
28 Ibid.

29 GRG/52/1/2/3/46,29/4/53, State Records of South Australia.
30 GRG/52/1/2/3/46, State Records of South Australia. See also Peggy Brock
    and Tom Gara, 'From segregation to Self-determination', in Peggy Brock
    and Tom Gara (eds), *Colonialism and Its Aftermath: A history of Aboriginal
    South Australia,* Adelaide: Wakefield Press, 2017, 47–50.
31 GRG/52/1/34/52, State Records of South Australia.
32 GRG/52/1/2/8/48, State Records of South Australia.
33 GRG/52/1/30/11/48, State Records of South Australia.
34 GRG/52/1, State Records of South Australia.
35 For example, Clem Coulthard, Rufus Wilton.
36 For example, Elsie Jackson, Roma Wilton, John McKenzie.
37 GRG/52/1/16/1/48, State Records of South Australia.
38 Ibid.
39 Rufus Wilton, personal communication; C.P. Mountford, fieldnotes.
40 GRG/52/1/16/1/48, State Records of South Australia.
41 Cliff Coulthard, personal communication.
42 Rufus Wilton, personal communication.

1973-2018 Self-determination and Native Title

1   Bob Ellis who was head of the Head of the Branch helped facilitate the
    creation of these positions. He did and continues to have a close working
    relationship with the Adnyamathanha.
2   http://www.mobilelanguageteam.com.au/languages/about/adnyamathnaha
3   Dorothy Tunbridge, *Flinders Ranges Dreaming,* Canberra: Aboriginal
    Studies Press, 1988
4   Lily Neville, *Adnyamathanha Ngawarla,* Collingwood, Vic: Australians
    Against Racism, 2008.
5   http://www.mobilelanguageteam.com.au/languages/about/adnyamathnaha
6   Christine Davis and Pearl McKenzie,*Adnyamathanha Genealogy,* Adelaide:
    Aboriginal Heritage Branch, Department of Environment and Planning,
    South Australia, 1985
7   Peggy Brock and Tom Gara (eds), *Colonialism and Its Aftermath: A history of
    Aboriginal South Australia*, Adelaide: Wakefield Press, 2017, 59.
8   http://www8.austlii.edu.au/cgi-bin/viewdoc/au/cases/cth/FCA/2009/359.
    html.
9   *Yura Nguthanha: Our Story, Our Vision, Our Way 2018–2022*, Port Augusta:
    ATLA, 2018.
10 Introduction by Damian Coulthard in *Adnyamathanha Traditional Lands
    Association Annual Report 2016/17*, pp. 2, 16.
11 *Yura Nguthanha: Our Story, Our Vision, Our Way 2018–2022*, ATLA, 2018.
12 http://leighcreekfutures.sa.gov.au/
13 http://www.abc.net.au/news/2018–09–18/aboriginal-bid-to-stop-
    controversial-gas-project-fails/10268134.

14 Giles Hamm, Vincent Coulthard, Cliff Coulthard et al., 'Cultural innovation and megafauna interaction in the early settlement of arid Australia', *Nature* vol 539, November 2016, 1.

15 *Yura Muda-Yura Yarta Yura Treaty*, ATLA, nd, 2.

16 http://www.industryandskills.sa.gov.au

17 Interview with Peggy Brock 1 August 2018. For another account of generational change among the Adnyamathanha see Pauline McKenzie, 'Life Story' in Peggy Brock and Tom Gara (eds), *Colonialism and Its Aftermath*, 261–64.

Bibliography

Primary Sources

NEWSPAPERS
Port Augusta Dispatch 1878, 1882
South Australian Register 1840–42, 1850, 1860

ARCHIVAL SOURCES
Beltana Police Station, Journal and Letterbook, GRG/5, State Records of South Australia

J.B. Bull, Reminiscences 1835–94, PRG 507/3, State Library of South Australia.

Commissioner of Police's Office, Correspondence files, GRG/5, State Records of South Australia

Mount Freeling Police Station, Journal, GRG/5, State Records of South Australia

Mountford-Sheard collection, Flinders Ranges Notebooks, State Library of South Australia

Police Officers' records, SA Police Department Archives

Port Augusta Police Station, Letterbook, GRG/5, State Records of South Australia

South Australian Aborigines Department, Correspondence files, GRG/52, State Records of South Australia

South Australian Chief Secretary's Office, Correspondence files GRG/24, State Records of South Australia

South Australian Lands Department, Mount Serle Station, 1324/14, State Records of South Australia

South Australian Museum Archives Accession No. 162, 642, 2286

South Australian Protector of Aborigines, Correspondence received, Outletter book, Reports, GRG/52, State Records of South Australia

PARLIAMENTARY AND DEPARTMENTAL SOURCES
Report of the Select Committee of the Legislative Council Upon the Aborigines SA Government 1860
South Australian Government Gazette 1856–66, 1874, 1878
South Australian Lands Department, maps and plans Mount Serle 1855, 1860, 1865, 1930–39
South Australian Parliamentary Papers 1858–59, 1887, 1891

Secondary Sources

Basedow, H., 'Burial Customs in the Northern Flinders Ranges of South Australia' in *Man*, No. 26, 1913.

Bell, Dianne and Ditton, Pam, *Law The Old and The New. Aboriginal Women in Central Australia Speak Out* Canberra: Central Australian Aboriginal Legal Service, 1980.

Brock, Peggy and Gara, Tom (eds), *Colonialism and Its Aftermath: A history of Aboriginal South Australia*, Adelaide: Wakefield Press, 2017.

Bruce, Robert, *Reminiscences of an old Squatter*, Adelaide: W.K. Thomas & Co., Printers, 1902. (1853) Facsimile copy 1973.

Bull, J.W., *Early Experiences of Colonial Life in South Australia*, Adelaide: Advertiser, Chronicle and Express Offices, 1878.

Cockburn, R., *Pastoral Pioneers of South Australia*, Vols. 1 and 2, facsimile edition, Blackwood, SA: Lynton Publications, 1974.

Curr, E.M., *The Australian Race* Vol. 2, Melbourne: John Ferres, Government Printer, 1886.

Davis, Christine and McKenzie, Pearl, *Adnyamathanha Geneaology*, Adelaide: Aboriginal Heritage Branch, Department of Environment and Planning, South Australia, 1985.

Dowling, Peter, 'Violent Epidemics: Disease, conflict and Aboriginal population collapse as a result of European contact in the Riverland of South Australia' MA thesis, ANU, Canberra, 1990

Elkin, A.P.,'Civilized Aborigines and Native Culture' in *Oceania*, Vol. 6 (2), Dec. 1935.

Ellis, R., 'Aboriginal Man in the Ranges' in *The Future of the Flinders Ranges* Proceedings of a Seminar, Department of Adult Education, Adelaide 1972.

Ellis, R., 'The Funeral Practices and Beliefs of the Adnjamathanha' in *Journal of the Anthropological Society of SA*, Vol. 13, (6), 1975.

Foster, Robert, 'Feasts of the Full-Moon: the distribution of rations to

Aborigines in South Australia, 1836–1861' *Aboriginal History* 13 (1), 1989, 63–78.

Gale, Fay, *A Study of Assimilation: Part Aborigines in South Australia*,Adelaide: Libraries Board of South Australia, 1964.

Gale, Fay, 'The History of Contact in South Australia' in J.W. Warburton (ed.), *Aborigines of South Australia: Their Background and Future Prospects* Adelaide: Department of Adult Education, 1969.

Gibbs, R.M., 'Humanitarian Theories and the Aboriginal Inhabitants of South Australia to 1860', Honours Thesis, Department of History, Adelaide, 1959.

Gillen, F.J. *Gillen's Diary: The Camp Jottings of F.J. Gillen on the Spencer and Gillen Expedition Across Australia 1901–1902,* Adelaide: Libraries Board of South Australia, 1968.

Hale, Herbert M. and Tindale, Norman B., 'Observations on Aborigines of the Flinders Ranges, and Records of Rock Carvings and Paintings' in *Records of the South Australian Museum*, Vol. 3(1), 45–60, 1925.

Hassell, K.L., 'The Relations between Settlers and Aborigines in South Australia', M.A. Thesis, Department of History, University of Adelaide, 1927.

Hayward, J.E., 'Diary 1846–56' in *Royal Geographical Society of Australia, South Australian Branch*, Vol. 29, 1927.

Hemmings, Steven, 'Conflict between Aborigines and Europeans along the Murray River from the Darling to the Great South Bend (1830–1841)', Honours Thesis, Department of History, Adelaide, 1982.

Heritage Unit, Department for the Environment, *The Flinders Ranges. An Aboriginal View*, Adelaide: The Department for the Environment, 1980.

Heritage Unit, Department for the Environment, *Minerawuta (Ram Paddock Gate)*, Adelaide: Department for the Environment, 1980.

Hull, I.V., *The Rise and Fall of Beltana,* Adelaide, 1973.

Jacobs, J.M., 'Aboriginal Land Rights in Pt. Augusta', M.A. Thesis, Department of Geography, University of Adelaide, 1983.

Jones, Philip, *Ochre and Rust: Artefacts and encounters on Australian frontiers,* Adelaide: Wakefield Press, 2007.

Lockwood, Christine, 'Early Encounters on the Adelaide Plains and Encounter Bay' in Peggy Brock and Tom Gara (eds), *Colonialism and Its Aftermath: A history of Aboriginal South Australia*, Adelaide, Wakefield Press, 2017.

McLean, J., 'Police Experience with the Natives Reminiscences of the Early Days of the Colony' in *Royal Geographical Society of Australia, South Australian Branch*, Vol. 6, 1903.

Mincham, Hans, *The Story of the Flinders Ranges,* Adelaide: Rigby, 1977.

Mountford, C.P. and Harvey, Alison, 'Women of the Adnjamathanha Tribe of the Northern Flinders Ranges' in *Oceania*, Vol. 12, Dec. 1941.

Neville, Lily, *Adnyamathanha Ngawarla*, Collingwood, Vic: Australians Against Racism, 2008.

Richardson, Norman A., *The Pioneers of the North-West of South Australia 1856–1914*, Adelaide: Thomas, 1925.

Ross, Betty, *Minerawuta (Ram Paddock Gate)*, Adelaide: Heritage Unit, SA Department for the Environment, 1981.

Schebeck, B., *Texts on the Social System of the Atynyamatana People with Grammatical Notes* Canberra: Dept. of Linguistics, Research School of Pacific Studies, Australian National University, 1974.

Schebeck, B., Hercus, L.A., White, M., *Papers in Australian Linguistics,* No. 6, Canberra: Pacific Linguistics Series A, No. 36, 1973.

Tindale, Norman B., *Aboriginal Tribes of Australia*, Canberra: Australian National University Press, 1974.

Tolmer, Alexander, *Reminiscences of an Adventurous and Chequered Career at Home and at the Antipodes,* London: Sampson Low, Marston, Searle & Rivington, 1882.

Tunbridge, Dorothy, *Flinders Ranges Dreaming*, Canberra: Aboriginal Studies Press, 1988.

Turner, V.E., *Pearls from the Deep. The Story of the Colebrook Home for Aboriginal Children, Quorn*, Adelaide: United Aborigines' Mission, 1936.

Woolmington, Jean (ed.), *Aborigines in Colonial Society: 1788–1850 From Noble Savage to Rural Pest*, Melbourne: Cassell Australia, 1973).

Yura Newsletter, Vol. I, Adelaide: Aboriginal Heritage Section, Department of Environment and Planning, 1977–78.

Yura Muda-Yura Yarta Yura Treaty, ATLA, nd, 2.

Yura Nguthanha: Our Story, Our Vision, Our Way 2018–2022, Port Augusta: ATLA, 2018.

Acknowledgements

The researching and writing of this book was assisted by the willing cooperation of a wide range of people and institutions. I would like to thank the many members of the Adnyamathanha community who contributed their time and knowledge including Rufus Wilton, the late Bill Stubbs, John McKenzie, Pearl McKenzie, Violet Gilbert, Claude Demell, Ethel Demell, Artie Wilton, Annie Coulthard, Roma Wilton, Gertie Johnson, Don Coulthard, Clem Coulthard, Cliff Wilton, Gladys Wilton, Willie Austen, Clara Coulthard and Elsie Jackson. I would also like to thank Philip Jones and the staff of the Australian Ethnology section of the archives, Jennifer Holt of the State Library for arranging access to the Mountford-Sheard collection, and the staff of the SA Archives for their friendly assistance.

I would particularly like to thank Vlad Potezny for his help in recording and documenting the Aboriginal sites identified in this study, and preparing the preliminary maps for publication, and the Department of Environment and Planning Drawing Office for producing the final maps. I would also like to thank the other staff of the Aboriginal Heritage Section for their advice and assistance, in particular, Cliff Coulthard, Des Coulthard, Christine Davis, Jo Bramley and Rosemary Buchan, and the Department of Environment and Planning library staff for their assistance with inter-library loans.

Peggy Brock

1985

Index

Wakefield Press is an independent publishing and
distribution company based in Adelaide, South Australia.
We love good stories and publish beautiful books.
To see our full range of books, please visit our website at
wakefieldpress.com.au
where all titles are available for purchase.

Find us!

Twitter: www.twitter.com/wakefieldpress
Facebook: www.facebook.com/wakefield.press
Instagram: instagram.com/wakefieldpress

www.ingramcontent.com/pod-product-compliance
Lightning Source LLC
Chambersburg PA
CBHW030842090426
42737CB00009B/1074